ALSO BY MARION CUNNINGHAM

The Fannie Farmer Cookbook
(with Jeri Laber)

The Fanny Farmer Baking Book

The Supper Book

Cooking With Child

English Bread & Yeast Cookery

The Maple Syrup Cookbook

Compliments of the Chef

THE BREAKFAST BOOK

Marion Cunningham

THE

BREAKFAST

BOOK

Illustrated by Donnie Cameron

WINGS BOOKS

New York • Avenel, New Jersey

This 1997 edition is published by Wings Books,
a division of Random House Value Publishing, Inc.,
201 East 50th Street, New York, N. Y. 10022,
by arrangement with Alfred A. Knopf, Inc.

Wings Books and colophon are trademarks of Random House Value Publishing, Inc.

Random House
New York • Toronto • London • Sydney • Auckland
http://www.randomhouse.com/

Printed and bound in the United States of America

Library of Congress Cataloging-in-Publication Data
Cunningham, Marion.
The breakfast book / Marion Cunningham : illustrated
by Donnie Cameron.
p. cm.
Reprint. Originally published: New York : Knopf, 1987.
Includes index.
ISBN 0-517-18726-4
1. Breakfasts. 2. Menus. I. Title.
TX 733.C83 1997   96-47642
641.5'2—dc21   CIP
8 7 6 5 4 3 2 1

This book is dedicated to my husband, Robert,

and children, Catherine and Mark.

Acknowledgments

My lasting appreciation to the following friends who gave their time and talent so generously to *The Breakfast Book*:

E. M. Ginger	Jim Dodge
Fritz Streiff	Abby Mandel
Helen Gustafson	Elaine Sherman
Loni Kuhn	Jacquie Lee
Sharon Kramis	Clark Wolfe

A special word: I thank John Hudspeth for his great taste and help and for bringing the breakfast dream alive through Bridge Creek Restaurant.

Contents

Introduction

As my interest in breakfast intensified over the last few years, I became more and more inspired to write this book. I have found that there are almost no books on the subject – no tempting recipes and nothing to encourage people to cook breakfast. There are lots of brunch books, but brunch, with its undefined ingredients and preparations, is entirely different from breakfast – it could be any meal. Brunch is almost always a partylike affair, served with wine and liquor, and with an assortment of unrelated dishes. Breakfast, on the other hand, involves no alcohol and usually consists of grains, dairy products, fruits, and maybe eggs or a little meat or fish.

I often ask people what they think of breakfast, and most reply instantly that it is their favorite meal. When pressed to tell what they eat for breakfast, their answers become rather vague. I've decided that they love the *idea* of breakfast, but they need some good guidance and recipes actually to get them to cook it. Breakfast has remained pure amid all the food trends with their stylish dishes and chic ingredients. The honest simplicity of breakfast is so captivating. The most delicious breakfasts usually derive from the humblest of ingredients (money alone does not buy good food).

The deeper reason that breakfast inspires me is that we have become so busy maintaining our lives in the working world that we often find ourselves sharing the same house with strangers. The meaning of "home" has disappeared. Surveys report that families no longer sit down together for the evening meal. Eating is a lonely experience for many, and we can be lonely without even knowing it sometimes. Standing up by a microwave oven, or refrigerator, or in front of the TV, automatically eating, leaves out a precious human element from our lives. Since when are business meetings, community gatherings, or basketball practice more important than talking with the people you care about and getting to know them better. If it is true that dinner is becoming a solitary, fast-feed-yourself experience, I'm hoping that breakfast, with its easy, wholesome honesty, will be an opportunity to be with and share oneself with friends and family. There is no greater inducement to conversation than sitting around a table and sharing a good meal. Gathering at the table for breakfast allows us to weave our lives with others — and that should be a daily pleasure.

More than ever, health has our attention these days. What we should and shouldn't eat, how to achieve good physical health, salt or no salt, sugar or no sugar ... But we tend to overlook one of the healthiest parts of eating: that it is such a wonderful means of bringing people together. My sense of health is that getting a good start with breakfast makes it the most important meal of the day. After the night's abstinence, it is important to break fast and eat a nutritious meal. Lunch may be only a token meal, and dinner or supper a modest one, but before expending energy for the day, food is essential. As tired as the old adage "moderation in all things" may be, I'm of the mind that we should follow this edict, and not become too anxious about each and every bite. I believe we should eat a wide variety of foods, without eating too much of any of them.

THE BREAKFAST BOOK

Yeast Breads

Breakfast isn't breakfast without bread, and yeast breads possess a sturdiness and strength that quick breads just don't have. Quick breads can be delicious and lively with lots of variations of flavor and texture, but compared to yeast breads they seem like adolescents next to their parents. More than any other kind of cooking I know of, making yeast bread can give you an almost primitive sense that you can take care of yourself and survive. And yeast bread for breakfast is so sustaining and welcoming. Once you've made your first loaf, you're apt to be hooked.

When I started baking with yeast, I thought it was much more complicated to use than it really is. If you are plunging in and using yeast for the first time, I suggest you start out with the Crisp Whole Wheat Buns on page 18. This is a simple and almost foolproof recipe: you just stir it up and watch it rise. The kneadings, risings, and punchings-down called for in the other recipes are mostly means to obtain a smoother and more uniform texture.

You need to know only a few things about yeast. Too much heat will kill it (the liquid should not be more than 105°F), and cool temperatures slow it down. Once you have mixed up your dough, you can interrupt and retard the fermentation process at any point by covering and refrigerating your dough for up to 24 hours; this gives you a lot of leeway.

Cooking is one of the legacies we can leave to the future, and I would like to be remembered for my baking. We all know we're not immortal, but after I'm gone, I would like my son and daughter to be able to say, "Our mother made real yeast bread for breakfast."

Basic American White Bread

(two medium loaves)

Many people like white toast for breakfast. It seems exactly right with a bowl of oatmeal or cold cereal. And plain white toast often tastes better with jams than whole grain breads do. American white bread usually has a little fat, a little sugar, and some milk in the recipe. These ingredients give the loaves keeping qualities which help preserve flavor and moistness.

½ cup warm water	2 tablespoons butter, shortening,
2 packages dry yeast	or oil, room temperature
1 teaspoon sugar	2 teaspoons salt
2 cups warm water	5 cups all-purpose flour,
½ cup nonfat dry milk	approximately

Put the ½ cup warm water in a large mixing bowl; sprinkle in the yeast and sugar, stir, and let dissolve for 5 minutes.

Add the 2 cups warm water, nonfat dry milk, butter, salt, and 2 cups of the flour to the yeast mixture. Using an electric mixer or a large spoon, beat the dough until it is smooth. Add only enough additional flour to make a manageable dough. At this point, knead with your hands on a lightly floured board for about 2 minutes, or use a dough hook in your electric mixer for about 15 seconds. Let the dough rest for 10 minutes. Resume kneading until the dough is smooth and elastic.

Put the dough in a greased bowl and cover with plastic wrap, and let it rise until double in bulk. Punch down and divide the dough in half.

Shape the dough and place in two greased 8½ × 4½ × 3-inch loaf pans. Loosely cover and let rise to the top of the pans.

Preheat the oven to 350°F. Bake for about 40 minutes, or until the loaves have shrunk away from the sides of the pans a trifle. Remove and cool on racks.

Cinnamon Swirl Bread After the dough has been punched down, divide the dough in half and pat each half into a piece that is about 8 inches square. Combine ½ cup sugar in a small bowl with 5 teaspoons cinnamon. Sprinkle the sugar mixture over each square of dough. Roll each piece of the dough into a tube shape and place in a greased loaf pan. Bake as directed above.

Dairy Bread

(two plump round loaves)

Milk and cottage cheese give this bread a pure dairy taste. The texture is rather springy, but soft. The addition of ¼ teaspoon of ground ginger follows an interesting old notion that ginger or cumin added in very tiny amounts to the dissolving yeast helps the yeast to do its work more effectively.

½ cup warm water
2 packages dry yeast
¼ teaspoon ground ginger
1 teaspoon plus 2 tablespoons
    sugar
1½ cups milk, warmed

1 cup cottage cheese
2 tablespoons butter, room
    temperature
1½ teaspoons salt
6 cups all-purpose flour,
    approximately

Put the warm water, yeast, ginger, and 1 teaspoon sugar in a large mixing bowl. Stir and let the mixture dissolve for 5 minutes.

Add the milk, cottage cheese, butter, the remaining 2 tablespoons sugar, salt, and 3 cups flour. Beat the mixture until it is smooth. Add only enough additional flour to make the dough manageable. Turn the dough onto a floured board or use the dough hook on an electric mixer to knead. Knead with your hands for 2 minutes or for 15 seconds with the dough hook. Let the dough rest for 10 minutes. Resume kneading until the dough is smooth and elastic.

Place the dough in a greased bowl and cover with plastic wrap. Let the dough double in bulk (this dough will rise faster than most, in about 1 hour). Punch down and divide the dough in half. Form two round loaves and place them on a greased baking sheet; or grease two 9- × 5- × 3-inch loaf pans and place the dough in these. Cover loosely and let rise for 45 minutes to 1 hour. Sprinkle a little flour on top and cut two slits or a cross on the top of each loaf.

Place in a preheated 375°F oven and bake for 40 to 50 minutes, or until the bread is golden on top. Cool on racks.

Granola Breakfast Bread

(two medium loaves)

This is my favorite bread. I eat a toasted slice almost every single morning for breakfast.

½ cup warm water	1 cup cornmeal
2 packages dry yeast	2 cups whole wheat bread flour
2 cups warm water	3 cups all-purpose flour,
½ cup nonfat dry milk	approximately
2 tablespoons butter	2 cups Granola (see page 90)
1½ teaspoons salt	

Put the ½ cup warm water in a mixing bowl; sprinkle the yeast over, stir, and let stand to dissolve for 5 minutes. Add the 2 cups warm water, nonfat dry milk, and butter, and stir to blend. Beat in the salt, cornmeal, and whole wheat bread flour and mix until smooth. Add 2 cups all-purpose flour and beat until well mixed. Beat in as much more flour as is needed to make a manageable dough. Add the granola.

Turn the dough onto a floured board (or use a dough hook on the electric mixer) and knead for a minute. Let the dough rest 10 minutes. Resume kneading until the dough is elastic, about 5 more minutes. Put the dough into a greased bowl and turn to coat all sides. Cover and let rise to double its bulk. Punch the dough down and divide in half. Put the dough into two greased 8½ × 4½ × 3-inch loaf pans. Let rise to the tops of the pans. Bake in a preheated 350°F oven for 45 minutes, or until lightly browned and done. Cool on racks.

Rusk or Zwieback

(two medium loaves)

Rusk or zwieback is a light yeast bread that has been sliced and slowly rebaked until golden and crisp throughout (zwieback is old German for "twice baked"). A rusk used to be considered the ideal toast for an infant or invalid, digestible and nourishing, but more important, rusk or zwieback is very satisfying for breakfast, with fruit or hot cereal.

½ cup warm water	1½ teaspoons salt
2 packages dry yeast	1½ tablespoons sugar
1½ cups milk, warmed	4½ cups all-purpose flour,
2 tablespoons butter	approximately

Put the warm water in a large mixing bowl, sprinkle the yeast over, and let stand to dissolve for 5 minutes.

Add the warm milk and butter to the yeast mixture and stir in the salt, sugar, and 2 cups flour. Stir briskly to mix well. Add only enough additional flour to make the dough manageable. Knead, using either an electric mixer with a dough hook or your hands, until the dough is smooth and elastic.

Divide the dough in half and shape each half into a roll 9 inches long and 2½ inches wide. Place each roll on a greased baking sheet. Cover loosely with plastic wrap and allow to double in bulk.

Preheat the oven to 375°F. Bake for 40 to 45 minutes, or until the tops are brown. Remove from the oven and cool on racks.

At this point you may freeze one loaf and slice the other. Each loaf will provide about 14 slices of rusk. Slice the bread about ½ inch thick and place the slices, flat side down, on a baking sheet. Bake in a preheated 250°F oven for about 1 hour, or until the slices are light brown and completely dry and crisp throughout.

Cream and Sugar Rusk   Mix ¼ cup cream with 6 tablespoons sugar and brush the tops of the slices of rusk halfway through the second baking.

Spiced Rusk   Add ¼ teaspoon cinnamon or nutmeg to the cream and sugar and brush on the rusk as directed above.

What Hymns are sung, what praises said
For home made miracles of Bread?
LOUIS UNTERMEYER, "Food and Drink" (1932)

Raisin Cinnamon Wheat Bread

(two medium loaves or one round loaf)

Toast made with Raisin Cinnamon Wheat Bread always seems a little special. This recipe calls for 2 cups of raisins. This is important. If it's supposed to be a raisin bread, be generous with the raisins!

½ cup warm water
2 packages dry yeast
1 teaspoon granulated sugar
2 cups warm water
½ cup nonfat dry milk
6 tablespoons brown sugar
1 tablespoon cinnamon
1½ teaspoons salt

2 tablespoons butter
2½ cups whole wheat flour
2 cups raisins (use 1 cup golden
  raisins and 1 cup dark raisins,
  if you have both)
3 cups all-purpose flour,
  approximately

Put the ½ cup warm water in a mixing bowl and stir in the yeast and granulated sugar. Let stand to dissolve for 5 minutes.

Add the 2 cups water, nonfat dry milk, brown sugar, cinnamon, salt, butter, and whole wheat flour to the yeast mixture. Beat briskly until the batter is smooth. Add the raisins. Add only enough all-purpose flour to make a manageable dough. If kneading by hand, turn onto a floured board and knead for 2 minutes; if you are using an electric mixer with a dough hook, knead for 15 seconds. Let the dough rest for 10 minutes. Resume kneading until the dough is smooth and elastic.

Put the dough in a greased bowl and cover with plastic wrap. Let the dough double in bulk. Punch the dough down. If you are making two loaves, divide the dough in half, shape into two loaves, and place in two greased 8½ × 4½ × 3-inch loaf pans. If you are making one loaf, roll it into a smooth ball, place on a greased baking sheet, and, using a sharp knife, cut two slashes across the top. Let the dough rise, loosely covered, for 45 minutes.

Put the loaves (or loaf) in a preheated 375°F oven. Bake for about 45 minutes, or until done; the round loaf will take 10 minutes longer. Remove from the oven and turn onto a rack to cool.

Dried Fruit Batter Bread

(one large loaf or two small loaves)

Even though it is made with yeast, Dried Fruit Batter Bread is fast to make and quite delicious. If you get about an hour's headstart, you can make it fresh for breakfast because this recipe is so simple. Batter breads tend to get stale more quickly than kneaded yeast breads, but if you freeze the unused bread immediately, the freshness will be preserved.

1/2 cup warm water	1 1/2 teaspoons salt
1 package dry yeast	1 egg
1 teaspoon plus 1/3 cup sugar	3 cups all-purpose flour
1 cup warm water	1 1/2 cups chopped dried fruit
4 tablespoons (1/2 stick) butter, room temperature	(prunes, apricots, figs, or a mixture)

Put the 1/2 cup warm water, yeast, and 1 teaspoon sugar in a large mixing bowl. Stir to blend and let stand for 5 minutes to dissolve the yeast.

Add the 1 cup warm water, butter, 1/3 cup sugar, salt, egg, and 1 cup flour. Beat the mixture vigorously until smooth. Add the remaining 2 cups flour and beat again until smooth. Add the dried fruit.

Pour the batter into a greased 9 × 5 × 3-inch pan or two 5 × 3 × 3-inch pans, loosely cover with plastic wrap, and let stand until doubled in bulk or until risen to the top of the pan.

Preheat the oven to 375°F. Bake the bread for 35 minutes if you are baking two small loaves; or 45 minutes if baking one large loaf. Remove from the oven, turn out of the pan, and cool on a rack.

Sally Lunn

(one medium loaf, or ten buns, or one 10-inch tube loaf)

Ever so simple, and faintly sweet with a tender crumb, Sally Lunn breads will round out any breakfast menu. The ease with which you can make these light, yellow breads makes them a fine breakfast basic. And they are versatile—they can be served with sweetened whipped cream and sliced berries or fruit. Sally Lunn toast is also very good.

½ cup warm water	½ cup (1 stick) butter, melted
2 packages dry yeast	4 eggs, room temperature
1 teaspoon plus ¼ cup sugar	1 teaspoon salt
½ cup heavy cream, warmed	3¾ cups all-purpose flour

Put the warm water in a large mixing bowl. Sprinkle the yeast and 1 teaspoon of sugar over, stir, and let stand to dissolve for 5 minutes.

Add the cream, butter, and eggs. Beat briskly until the mixture is well blended. Add the salt, remaining ¼ cup sugar, and 2 cups flour. Beat vigorously until the batterlike dough is smooth. Add the remaining flour and beat again until smooth. You can easily do this by hand, or with an electric mixer. Leave the dough in the mixing bowl but gather it into a ball off the sides of the bowl, cover the bowl with plastic wrap, and let the dough double in bulk. This will take about 2 hours.

Generously butter the pan or pans (I often make small buns, using muffin tins). Lightly flour your hands (the dough is a little sticky and "stretchy"). Then for buns, tear off pieces and fill the tins about two-thirds full; or place the dough in a loaf or tube pan. Cover and again let double in bulk: the dough should rise to the top of the tins or pans.

Preheat the oven to 350°F. Bake the buns for about 25 minutes. A loaf will take about 40 minutes, and a large tube bread about 50 minutes. Let cool 5 minutes in the pan, then turn out onto a rack to cool.

Oatmeal Orange Bread

(two medium loaves)

Freshly chopped orange and oatmeal make a very nice match. Try the variation recipe below for Orange Marmalade Oatmeal Bread: the additional step of spreading marmalade over the almost-baked loaves gives the bread a little extra sparkle.

½ cup warm water
1 teaspoon plus 2 tablespoons
  sugar
2 packages dry yeast
1¼ cups milk, warmed
2 tablespoons butter, room
  temperature
1½ teaspoons salt

2 cups cooked oatmeal
5 cups all-purpose flour,
  approximately
1 orange, quartered, seeded,
  and ground in a food processor
  or coarsely chopped (to make
  1 cup)

Put the ½ cup warm water and 1 teaspoon sugar in a large mixing bowl; add the yeast, stir, and let stand to dissolve for 5 minutes.

Add the milk, butter, salt, remaining 2 tablespoons sugar, oatmeal, and 2 cups flour to the yeast mixture. Stir briskly until well mixed. Add only enough additional flour to make a manageable dough. Add the ground orange. Knead the dough for 1 minute by hand, or if you are using an electric mixer with a dough hook, for 15 seconds. Let the dough rest for 10 minutes. Resume kneading until the dough is smooth and elastic.

Put the dough in a greased bowl, cover with plastic wrap, and let double in bulk. Punch the dough down and divide in half. Put each half in a greased 8½ × 4½ × 3-inch loaf pan and allow to rise to the tops of the pans.

Bake in a preheated 375°F oven for about 45 minutes, or until done. Remove from the oven and turn onto racks to cool.

Orange Marmalade Bread Quarter, seed, and grind (in a food processor) or coarsely chop enough orange to make 1 cup. Cook with 1 cup sugar until the sugar melts and the marmalade looks shiny (about 5 minutes). Cool and spread half of the marmalade on top of each loaf 10 minutes before the bread is done.

Orange Rye Bread

(one medium loaf and ten rolls)

Rye and orange go together like ham and eggs. This makes good toast that is even better with orange marmalade.

2 packages dry yeast
1/2 cup warm water
1 teaspoon plus 1 tablespoon
  sugar
2 cups rye flour
1 tablespoon caraway seeds
2 tablespoons finely chopped or
  grated orange zest

1 teaspoon salt
1 cup milk, warmed
2 tablespoons shortening
1 egg
1 1/2 cups all-purpose flour,
  approximately

Sprinkle the yeast over the warm water in a large mixing bowl, stir in 1 teaspoon sugar, and let stand to dissolve for 5 minutes.

Add the rye flour, caraway seeds, orange zest, and salt; then add the milk, remaining tablespoon sugar, shortening, and egg, beating well to mix. Slowly add only enough all-purpose flour to make a manageable dough. Knead the dough by hand on a floured board for about 6 to 8 minutes, or with an electric mixer that has a dough hook. Rye flour never gets smooth and elastic the way wheat flour does, so don't worry about the dough remaining a little tacky—it is the nature of rye flour.

Place the dough in a greased bowl and cover with plastic wrap. Let double in bulk. Punch down and divide the dough in half. Place one half in a greased 8½ × 4½ × 3-inch loaf pan. Divide the remaining half into 10 equal pieces and roll each one into a ball. Place balls an inch apart on a greased baking sheet. Loosely cover the loaf and rolls with plastic wrap and let rise about 1 hour.

Preheat the oven to 375°F. Bake the loaf for about 45 minutes and the rolls 25 to 30 minutes.

Mexican Bread

(two large loaves)

This is a wonderful bread full of the clear, snappy flavors of pepper and cheese with a slightly coarse texture from the cornmeal. Make breakfast sandwiches with this bread, spread with cheese and fresh cilantro and grilled. Serve the sandwich with cold melon and hot Mexican Chocolate (see page 292).

½ cup warm water
2 packages dry yeast
1 cup yellow cornmeal
2 teaspoons salt
1 tablespoon sugar
½ teaspoon baking soda
2 eggs
1 cup buttermilk

½ cup vegetable oil
1 cup creamed corn
5 cups all-purpose flour, approximately
1½ cups grated sharp Cheddar cheese
¼ cup chopped mild green chilis (fresh or canned)

Put the warm water in a large mixing bowl and stir in the yeast. Let stand to dissolve for 5 minutes.

Add the cornmeal, salt, sugar, and baking soda and beat until well mixed. Add the eggs, buttermilk, oil, corn, and 2 cups flour. Beat vigorously until well blended. Add the cheese and chilis and more flour to make the dough manageable. Knead until the cheese and chilis are well distributed. Let the dough rest 10 minutes. Resume kneading until the dough becomes smooth and elastic. Put the dough into a greased bowl. Cover the bowl with plastic wrap and let stand until the dough doubles in bulk.

Punch down the dough. Divide the dough in half and form into two loaves. Place in two greased 9 × 5 × 3-inch loaf pans, cover lightly, and let rise to the tops of the pans. Bake in a preheated 350°F oven for 50 to 60 minutes. Remove from pans and cool on racks.

Chocolate Walnut Butter Bread

(two medium loaves)

Save this recipe for a very special breakfast. When you eat this buttery, tender-crumbed bread you encounter a wonderful array of rich, surprising tastes. Chocolate Walnut Butter Bread also makes extraordinary French toast—just be sure to dip the sliced bread into the egg only briefly so that the slices don't get soaked through.

½ cup warm water
1 package dry yeast
3½ cups all-purpose flour
1 tablespoon sugar
1¼ teaspoons salt
4 eggs, room temperature
12 tablespoons (1½ sticks) butter, softened

1 cup chopped (into large pieces) walnuts
6 ounces (6 squares) semisweet chocolate, broken or chopped into large pieces

Put the water in a large mixing bowl and sprinkle in the yeast. Stir and allow to stand for 5 minutes to dissolve.

Add the flour, sugar, salt, and eggs to the yeast mixture and beat vigorously until well blended. Beat in the butter in tablespoon-size pieces until it is all incorporated and the batter is smooth. Cover the bowl with plastic wrap and let the batter rise to double its bulk.

Stir the batter down and add the walnuts and chocolate pieces. Spoon the batter into two greased 8½ × 4½ × 3-inch loaf pans (the pans should be half full so the loaves will have nicely rounded tops when they finish baking). Bake in a preheated 350°F oven for about 45 minutes. Remove from the oven and allow to rest for 5 minutes, then turn loaves out onto racks.

Crisp Whole Wheat Buns

(one dozen buns)

No kneading is necessary for these crisp-crusted whole wheat buns. Split in half, toasted, and buttered, they are outstandingly good.

½ cup warm water	1 tablespoon sugar
2 packages dry yeast	2 cups whole wheat flour
1 cup warm water	1½ cups all-purpose flour
1 teaspoon salt	3 tablespoons yellow cornmeal

Put ½ cup warm water in a large mixing bowl and stir in the yeast. Let stand to dissolve 5 minutes.

Add the remaining cup warm water, salt, sugar, and 2 cups whole wheat flour. Using a mixing spoon, beat the dough vigorously for a minute or two. Add the all-purpose flour and beat until smooth. Cover the bowl with plastic wrap and let the dough rise until double in bulk (this happens quickly, in about 45 minutes). The dough will be rather sticky, so lightly flour your hands. Punch the dough down, then pull off about ⅓ cup dough at a time and shape into a ball.

Preheat the oven to 400°F. Sprinkle the yellow cornmeal over a baking sheet. Place the buns 1 inch apart on the baking sheet. Let the buns rest and rise slightly for 15 minutes. Sprinkle or spray cold water lightly over the buns (a plant mister is ideal), and place in the oven. After 15 minutes of baking, sprinkle or mist the tops of the buns once again with cold water (the water makes the crust crisper). Bake 10 minutes more, or until the buns are lightly browned on top. Remove and serve warm.

Breakfast Baps

(sixteen baps)

This is the Scot's breakfast roll. Crisp-crusted, soft-centered, and well buttered, a friendlier roll you'll never meet.

1 teaspoon sugar
1/3 cup warm water
3 packages dry yeast
4 cups all-purpose flour
1 1/2 teaspoons salt

1/2 cup lard or shortening
   (try to use lard—it lends a
   good "barny" taste)
1/2 cup milk, warmed
1/2 cup warm water

Dissolve 1 teaspoon sugar in a bowl with 1/3 cup warm water, sprinkle the yeast over, and stir. Let stand to dissolve for 5 minutes.

In another bowl mix the flour and salt and rub in the lard. Add the yeast mixture, then the milk and 1/2 cup water, and stir to mix. You want a soft dough. Use your hands to mix—it's easier. Cover the dough and let it rise for about an hour, or until double in bulk.

Turn the dough out onto a floured board and knead until smooth. Cut the dough into 16 pieces and form each piece into a small ball. Place the balls on a greased baking sheet. Allow to rise for 30 minutes.

Preheat the oven to 400°F. Bake the baps 20 to 25 minutes, or until golden brown. Serve hot.

Glazed Cinnamon Rolls

(two dozen round rolls)

These rolls are light but rich, with ample butter and modestly spiced — the amount of cinnamon is not overpowering. The shiny glaze finishes them in a pretty manner.

¼ cup warm water
1 package dry yeast
1 teaspoon plus ¼ cup sugar
4 cups all-purpose flour
1 teaspoon salt
½ pound (2 sticks) butter, chilled
3 egg yolks
1 cup milk

Filling
¼ cup (½ stick) butter, melted
6 tablespoons sugar
1 teaspoon cinnamon

Glaze
1½ cups confectioners' sugar
2 tablespoons butter, room
   temperature
1 tablespoon water (a trifle more
   may be needed to make a
   manageable glaze)

Put the warm water in a small bowl and sprinkle the yeast over. Add 1 teaspoon sugar, stir, and let dissolve for 5 minutes.

In a large mixing bowl, stir together the flour, ¼ cup sugar, and salt with a fork to mix them well. Cut the butter into pieces the size of small grapes and add to the flour mixture. Using either your hands or a pastry blender, rub or cut the butter into the flour mixture until it is distributed and there are coarse little lumps of butter throughout. Stir in the yeast mixture, the egg yolks, and milk. Beat until blended. Cover with plastic wrap and chill in the refrigerator at least 6 hours (this dough can be refrigerated for 12 to 14 hours).

Divide the dough in half. On a lightly floured board, roll out half the dough into a rectangle about 10 by 12 inches. Spread 2 tablespoons of the melted butter over the rectangle. Mix the remaining 6 tablespoons sugar and the 1 teaspoon cinnamon together in a small bowl. Sprinkle half the sugar mixture evenly over the rectangle. Starting with the wide side, roll up the rectangle like a jelly roll. Divide the roll into 12 pieces by first cutting the roll into 4 equal portions, then cutting each portion into 3. Put the rolls cut side down in a greased muffin tin. Repeat these steps with the other half of the dough. Cover loosely and let rise for 1 hour.

Bake in a preheated 400°F oven for 20 to 25 minutes. Remove the rolls and put them on a rack set over a piece of waxed paper.

To make the glaze, sift the confectioners' sugar into a small bowl, then beat in the butter and water until smooth. Spoon a little of the glaze over each roll while still hot.

Double-Proof Biscuits

(about four dozen biscuits)

Because leavening agents in the nineteenth century were often unreliable, cooks would often use more than one in the same recipe for insurance—which is undoubtedly how this recipe developed. Today, when yeast and baking powder are all sure-proof, combining them isn't necessary but it does make for a particularly ethereal biscuit. Appropriately, the old-fashioned name for these is angel biscuits.

1 package dry yeast	3 tablespoons sugar
½ cup warm water	¾ cup shortening
5 cups all-purpose flour	1 teaspoon baking soda
4 teaspoons baking powder	2 cups buttermilk
2 teaspoons salt	

Sprinkle the yeast over the water in a small bowl, stir, and let stand 5 minutes to dissolve.

In a large mixing bowl combine the flour, baking powder, salt, and sugar, and stir with a fork to mix. Add the shortening and cut into the flour mixture, either using your fingertips or a pastry cutter, until the mixture looks irregular and crumbly.

Add the baking soda to the buttermilk. Stir the buttermilk into the flour mixture. Add the yeast mixture. Mix well. Cover and refrigerate for about 8 hours.

Turn the dough onto a lightly floured board. Knead a dozen times. Roll dough out to about ½-inch thickness. Cut out the biscuits with a 2-inch cutter and place them 1 inch apart on greased baking pans. Cover and let rise for 1 hour.

Bake in a preheated 400°F oven for about 15 minutes, or until lightly browned. Serve hot.

Hot Cross Buns

(three dozen buns)

Hot Cross Buns symbolize the Easter season and are eaten on Good Friday (and other times, too). They are also the harbinger of spring for some of us. This recipe makes a mildly spiced bun with a scattering of currants and raisins.

½ cup warm water
2 packages dry yeast
1 teaspoon plus ½ cup sugar
1 cup warm water
½ cup nonfat dry milk
½ cup (1 stick) butter, melted
½ teaspoon salt
3 eggs, lightly beaten
6 cups all-purpose flour,
    approximately

¾ teaspoon cinnamon
¾ teaspoon allspice
1 cup raisins
½ cup currants

Glaze
1 cup confectioners' sugar
1 tablespoon hot water

Put the ½ cup warm water in a large mixing bowl and stir in the yeast and 1 teaspoon sugar. Let stand to dissolve for 5 minutes.

Add 1 cup warm water, dry milk, melted butter, the remaining ½ cup sugar, salt, and eggs. Beat briskly to blend well. Stir in 3 cups flour, cinnamon, and allspice and beat thoroughly. Add the raisins and currants. Beat in only enough additional flour to make a manageable dough.

Turn the dough onto a floured board and knead for 1 minute. Let the dough rest for 10 minutes. Resume kneading until the dough is smooth and elastic. Put the dough in a greased bowl, turn to coat the dough on all sides, cover with plastic wrap, and let double in bulk.

Punch the dough down and turn out onto a lightly floured board. Roll out the dough, or pat and stretch it, to a ½-inch thickness. Cut out the buns with a 2½-inch circular cutter. Grease two baking sheets. Make the buns by forming each dough round into a smooth ball, smoothing the underside of the ball and pinching and tucking away any loose ends. Place the buns 1 inch apart on the sheets. Let them rise for 1 hour.

Preheat the oven to 375°F. Bake for approximately 20 minutes, or until the buns are golden on top. Remove and cool slightly on racks.

To glaze the buns, combine the confectioners' sugar and water (this glaze should be medium thick), adding a trifle more water if too thick. Using either a pastry bag fitted with a ⅟16-inch tube, or a toothpick, apply the glaze in the shape of a cross on the top of each bun.

Sticky Buns

(two dozen buns)

Cinnamon and other spices have no place in these sticky buns—they have the seductive flavor of caramel and pure, sweet butter and the crunch of nuts.

½ cup warm water
2 packages dry yeast
2 cups milk, warmed
½ cup vegetable shortening
6 tablespoons sugar
2 teaspoons salt
2 eggs, room temperature
6½ cups all-purpose flour,
    approximately

Caramel Glaze
½ pound (2 sticks) butter
3 cups brown sugar
½ cup light corn syrup
3 cups broken pecan or walnut
    pieces

Put the water in a small bowl and sprinkle the yeast over. Stir and let stand for 5 minutes to dissolve.

Put the warm milk, shortening, sugar, salt, and eggs in a large mixing bowl and beat until well blended. Add the yeast and 4 cups flour. Mix vigorously. Add only enough flour to make a soft, manageable dough. Sprinkle a board with flour and turn the dough out onto it. Knead for 1 minute. Let the dough rest for 10 minutes. Resume kneading until the dough is smooth and elastic. Put the dough in a greased bowl, cover with plastic wrap, and let rise until double in bulk.

Make the caramel glaze. Put the butter, brown sugar, and corn syrup in a heavy-bottomed saucepan. Put the pan over medium heat and stir often until the butter is melted, the sugar is dissolved, and the mixture is well blended. Remove from the heat and pour 1 cup of the glaze into a small bowl. Set aside. Spread the remaining 2 cups glaze over the bottoms of three 8-inch cake pans. Sprinkle 1 cup pecans or walnuts over the glaze in each of the pans.

Punch the dough down and divide into thirds; while you work with one part, cover the remaining pieces of dough. Roll the first third of dough into a rectangle about 8 by 12 inches. Spread 1/3 cup of the caramel glaze that has been set aside over the rectangle. Loosely roll the rectangle from the wide side, making a long tube. Cut into eight pieces, each 1 1/2 inches thick. Place the rounds, flat side down, in one of the cake pans. Cover the pan loosely with plastic wrap. Repeat with each remaining third of the dough. Let the shaped dough rise for about 35 to 45 minutes, or until the dough looks a little puffy.

Preheat the oven to 375°F. Bake for 35 to 45 minutes, or until a straw comes out clean when inserted into the center bun — there should be no dough clinging to the straw. Invert the cake pans over racks with waxed paper underneath to catch dripping glaze. Serve warm.

CRUMPETS AND ENGLISH MUFFINS

One could spend weeks searching through food history books trying to define the exact differences between muffins and crumpets. Both English muffins and crumpets are made with yeast and baked in rings on a griddle, but they are somewhat different. I think of crumpets as being made from a batter that has a little baking soda dissolved in warm water added to it just before griddling. Baking soda helps create the honeycombed surface that characterizes the crumpet. Also, crumpets are baked on one side only and are thinner than English muffins.

English muffins are made of a soft yeast dough that is mixed, allowed to rise, turned onto a floured board, and just barely kneaded. They are shaped, left to rest on cornmeal for a bit, and then both sides are baked on the griddle.

Both English muffins and crumpets are easier and much quicker to make than other kinds of yeast breads — no kneading is necessary and only brief rising. It is important to know that crumpets and English muffins are not ready to eat until they are toasted.

If rings used for griddling crumpets and muffins are difficult to find, you can use 6½-ounce tin cans (the kind tuna fish comes in) with the tops and bottoms cut out.

Breakfast is a forecast of the whole day:
Spoil that and all is spoiled.
                                    LEIGH HUNT

Crumpets

(one dozen round crumpets)

Good crumpets are holey and spongy and are best eaten doused with butter and spread with honey or jam.

1 package dry yeast
¼ cup warm water
1 teaspoon sugar
1½ cups milk, warmed

2 cups all-purpose flour
1 teaspoon salt
½ teaspoon baking soda
¼ cup warm water

Sprinkle the yeast over the warm water in a mixing bowl. Add the sugar, stir, and let the yeast dissolve for 5 minutes. Add the milk, flour, and salt. Beat until smooth. Cover the bowl with plastic wrap and let stand for 1 hour (if you want to make the batter the night before, cover and refrigerate overnight). Stir down, dissolve the baking soda in ¼ cup warm water, and stir into the batter. Cover and let rest for 30 minutes.

Heat a griddle and grease some 3-inch rings (you can use 6½-ounce tuna-type cans with tops and bottoms cut out). When the griddle is medium hot, grease it and place the rings on it. Spoon about 3 tablespoons batter into each ring, just enough to cover the bottom. Lower the heat and cook slowly on the griddle for about 8 minutes, or until the tops of the crumpets have lost their shine and are dull and holey. Remove the rings and set aside the crumpets. When you've finished the batch, toast the crumpets, butter them generously, and serve.

English Muffins

(sixteen muffins)

Proof again that everything is best when baked at home. Crusty and pleasantly tough on the outside, tender and lavishly buttered on the inside, these should be on your agenda weekly.

½ cup warm water
1 package dry yeast
1½ teaspoons salt
1 tablespoon sugar
1 cup milk, warmed

3½ cups all-purpose flour
3 tablespoons vegetable oil or melted shortening
½ cup cornmeal

Pour the water into a large mixing bowl, sprinkle the yeast over, and stir. Let stand for 5 minutes to dissolve. Stir in the salt, sugar, warm milk, 2 cups flour, and the oil. Stir briskly with a spoon for a minute to mix well. Add the remaining flour and stir to blend smoothly. This dough will be very soft. Cover and let the dough double in bulk (it will take about an hour).

Flour a board and your hands. Put the dough on the board, and add a little flour if it is too sticky to manage. Knead the dough three or four times. Pat and push the dough out so it is about ¼ inch thick. Using a 3-inch ring (or a 6½-ounce tuna can with top and bottom cut out) as a cutter, cut the dough out and place the muffins 1 inch apart on a baking sheet that has been sprinkled with the cornmeal. When the muffins are all cut, cover them lightly with a towel and let them rest for 30 minutes. Heat a griddle until medium hot and film it with grease. Grease the inside of the rings and place on the griddle. Put the muffins in the rings and cook for 10 minutes on one side and 5 minutes on the other. Before serving, split the muffins in half with a fork and toast them. Butter generously and serve warm.

Toasts, French Toast, and Breakfast Sandwiches

Melba Toast
Pulled Bread
Milk Toast
   Stove Top
   Oven
Cinnamon Toast
Toasts
   Sausage Applesauce
   Apple and Cheese
   Ham
   Banana
   Tomato
   Mushroom
   Creamed Mushroom
   Smoked Salmon
Welsh Rabbit with Beer
Tomato Rabbit
French Toast
   Spiced
   Lemon or Orange
   Maple Syrup
   Fruit Syrup
   Buttermilk
J.B.'s French Toast
Breakfast Sandwiches
   Fig and Ham on Rye Bread
   Sausage and Melted Cheese
   Walnut Butter
   Date and Breakfast Cheese
   Strawberry
   Ham and Farm Cheese Butter-Fried
   Mexican Breakfast

For some of us, a complete breakfast can be toast all by itself. Toasting brings out bread's good qualities — when toasted, bread has a deep grainy flavor and an irresistible fragrance. There is nothing like the smell of bacon frying and bread toasting to hurry one to the breakfast table.

I think toast is best when it is evenly golden. If you ever take the time to toast bread under the broiler, you will agree that it's lots better than toast made in an electric toaster. Keep your butter spreadable so you can butter your toast right to the edges and have butter in every bite.

Melba Toast

Melba Toast was invented at the Ritz in Paris at the turn of the century for a dieting diva — the same Nellie Melba who gave her name to the peaches. Tea and Melba Toast make a harmonious duet.

You will need a frozen loaf of unsliced white bread (commercial or homemade) or Cinnamon Swirl Bread (see page 7). Homemade grain breads are too dense to slice thin enough for Melba Toast. Slice the frozen bread into 1/8-inch-thick slices and remove the crusts. Spread the slices on a baking sheet in a single layer and put into a preheated

225°F oven for 45 minutes, checking after 30 minutes. The bread should be lightly golden and very crisp and the edges of the slices will have curled up. Melba toast keeps indefinitely in an airtight container.

Pulled Bread

Either you're a crunchy person or you're not. If you like crunch, pulled bread is for you. To make it, you slowly toast a loaf of crustless bread that has been shredded apart into pieces just the right size for munching along with a piece of cheese or a spoonful of jam. This was a popular kind of dry toast in the eighteenth and nineteenth centuries, especially in hotel restaurants.

Preheat the oven to 250°F. Cut the crust from a loaf of unsliced bread (feed the crusts to the birds). Pull irregular-size pieces about 2 or 3 inches long from the loaf until it is all broken up. Spread the pieces on a baking sheet. Bake for about 1 hour, until the bread is dry, crisp, and golden. Remove from the oven, pile in a napkin-lined basket or dish, and serve. Pulled bread will keep almost indefinitely stored in an airtight container.

Milk Toast

Why in the world did we ever abandon milk toast? Although it sounds deceptively bland and dull, it isn't; and as the Victorians discovered, it can revive the peaked or sad. Nourishing and soul-satisfying, milk toast will banish the blues.

STOVE TOP   For each serving of the simplest of milk toasts, first lightly toast 2 slices of bread. Place the slices in a bowl. Pour 1½ cups milk into a saucepan, bring just to a boil, remove from the heat, and stir in 1½ tablespoons butter. If you like, add a tablespoon of sugar and a pinch of ground nutmeg. Pour the milk into the bowl over the bread. Cover, and let stand for 5 minutes—don't stir or you will spoil the texture. Serve hot.

OVEN   To make baked milk toast for two, preheat the oven to 350°F and butter a shallow baking dish that will hold four slices of bread in a single layer. Butter four slices of bread (preferably homemade and cut ¾ inch thick). Place the slices in one layer in the baking dish. Pour 1⅓ cups of milk over the bread and cover the baking dish (with foil if it has no lid). Bake for 30 minutes. Sometimes a light sprinkle of granulated sugar is just right on milk toast. Serve hot.

Cinnamon Toast

Though Cinnamon Toast comes and goes in one's life, it is always welcome as an old friend. For 2 slices of toast, first mix together in a small bowl 4 teaspoons sugar and ⅛ teaspoon cinnamon. Sprinkle 2 teaspoons of the cinnamon sugar over each buttered slice of lightly, freshly toasted bread. Place the toast under the broiler for about 1 minute (watch closely), or until the sugar has melted. Serve warm.

TOASTS

Old American cookbooks often have a chapter called The Toast Family or Divers Kinds of Toast with recipes for little garnished toasts as breakfast or lunch dishes. These modest-size meals on toast make a nice change from toast and sweet jam, and offer a little more nourishment and variety. Another nice thing about them is that they are practical and manageable if you get the notion to carry them back to bed.

Sausage Applesauce Toast

Lightly toast 2 slices rye bread and butter them right to the edges. Crumble about ¼ cup cooked sausage (if you want to try making your own sausage—and it's well worth the effort—follow the recipe for Breakfast Sausage on page 197) over each slice of toast and cover with ¼ cup applesauce. Put under the broiler for about 1 minute (watch carefully) or in a hot oven until the toast is very hot. Serve immediately.

Apple and Cheese Toast

For 2 pieces of toast, peel, core, and slice up an apple. Melt 2 tablespoons butter in a small skillet and add the apple slices. Cook over low heat for 3 or 4 minutes, or until the apple is tender. Set the apple aside. Sprinkle ⅓ cup grated Cheddar cheese over each of 2 buttered slices of fresh, lightly toasted bread. Place them under the broiler.

Keep an eye on them, and broil just until the cheese has melted. Arrange the apple slices over the melted cheese and serve warm.

Ham Toast

For 2 toasts, mix ⅔ cup cooked, ground ham, 3 tablespoons heavy cream, and ⅛ teaspoon nutmeg together in a small bowl. Butter 2 slices of fresh, lightly toasted bread and spread half the mixture over each one. Place the toasts in a hot oven or under the broiler until well heated. Serve hot.

Banana Toast

For 2 pieces of toast, peel a banana and cut in half, then slice each half lengthwise into 3 pieces. Melt 2 tablespoons butter in a small skillet over low heat. Put the banana slices in the skillet and cook over low heat for about 1 minute on each side. Butter 2 slices fresh whole wheat toast and put 3 slices of banana on each one. Stir together 1 teaspoon sugar and a pinch of nutmeg and sprinkle this over the banana slices. Serve warm.

Tomato Toast

For 2 pieces of toast, chop up enough fresh tomato to make about 1 cup and have ready 6 tablespoons fresh bread crumbs. Melt 1½ tablespoons butter in a skillet and stir in the bread crumbs. Lightly brown them over medium heat, stirring constantly. Remove the bread crumbs from the pan, mix in 1/4 teaspoon finely chopped fresh sage, and set aside. Add 1 1/2 tablespoons more butter to the skillet and stir in the tomato. Add salt and pepper to taste and cook for 1 minute, stirring constantly. Remove from the heat, spread the tomato mixture over 2 slices buttered toast, and sprinkle the bread crumbs and sage over the top. Serve warm.

Mushroom Toast

For 2 pieces of toast, prepare about 2 1/2 cups sliced mushrooms. Melt 4 tablespoons (1/2 stick) butter in a skillet over low heat. Stir in the mushrooms and continue to cook over low heat until the mushrooms soften a little. Salt lightly and pepper amply. Stir 2 teaspoons fresh lemon juice into the mushrooms, and spread them over 2 slices of fresh, light toast buttered right to the edges. Serve hot.

Creamed Mushroom Toast

For 2 slices of toast, you will need 1/2 pound medium-size mushrooms. Wipe them clean, remove the stems (save and add to an omelet), and slice the caps in half. Melt 3 tablespoons butter in a large skillet and add the mushrooms. Cook, stirring constantly, over medium heat only until they have darkened slightly. Add salt and pepper to taste. Then add 1/2 cup heavy cream and, if you like, 1 tablespoon dry sherry. Stir only until the mixture is well blended and hot. Spoon the creamed mushrooms over 2 slices of freshly toasted and buttered white bread. Garnish with flat-leaf Italian parsley.

Smoked Salmon Toast

On each slice of buttered rye toast, spread ¼ cup softened cream cheese. Sprinkle ½ teaspoon fresh or dried dill and a few drops of lemon juice over the cheese. Cover each piece of toast with a thin slice of smoked salmon and serve cold. Very compatible with a halved hard-boiled egg on the plate.

BREAKFAST IN BED

One of the most blissful escapes is breakfast in bed with something good to read. Breakfast in bed is cozy, quiet, and private. I instantly forget that it was I who fixed the tray. The simplest food tastes special. Since food that spills or sloshes can ruin the mood, this is the moment when toasts should be considered. A thermos of hot coffee or tea is ideal.

As one is softly propped up in bed the world falls away, and breakfast becomes what some poet called "a parenthesis in time."

M.C.

Welsh Rabbit with Beer

(four servings)

Welsh Rabbit is certainly a warm and comforting dish, the kind that clears the head and quiets the stomach.

2 tablespoons butter
2 tablespoons flour
1 cup beer or ale
1 teaspoon Worcestershire sauce
1 teaspoon dry mustard

Salt to taste
2 cups grated sharp Cheddar
  cheese
6 slices whole wheat or rye bread,
  toasted and buttered

Melt the butter in a skillet and add the flour, stirring constantly. Cook over medium-low heat until well blended, about 2 minutes. Slowly add the beer, stirring constantly, until thickened and smooth. Add the Worcestershire sauce, dry mustard, and salt and stir until smooth and blended. Add the cheese and cook, stirring until smooth and thick. Taste and correct seasonings.

Put 1½ slices of buttered toast on each plate. Spoon the Welsh Rabbit over the toast and serve hot.

Tomato Rabbit

(six servings)

½ cup finely chopped tomato
⅛ teaspoon baking soda
2 cups grated extra sharp
  Cheddar cheese
2 eggs, slightly beaten
1 teaspoon dry mustard

Cayenne pepper to taste
2 tablespoons butter
2 tablespoons flour
1 cup light cream
Salt to taste
6 slices toast, buttered

In a mixing bowl, stir together the tomatoes with the baking soda, cheese, eggs, mustard, and cayenne pepper. Melt the butter in a saucepan. Stir in the flour and cook for 2 to 3 minutes, stirring. Slowly pour in the cream and cook, stirring, until the mixture thickens. Add the tomato mixture to the sauce and cook over gentle heat, stirring constantly, until the cheese melts—do not boil. Taste and add salt if needed. Spoon over the toast and serve hot.

French Toast

(four servings)

French toast is so good that you forget how economical it is. The French don't call this French toast. They call it *pain perdu* or "lost bread," because it is a way to use up leftover bread you would otherwise lose—the only bread you've got on the baker's day off. French toast is actually better if the bread is a little old or sliced and dried out overnight.

3 eggs	6 slices bread (preferably a
¾ cup milk, light cream, or	dense homemade type;
heavy cream	typically white, but try rye or
Salt to taste	whole wheat, too)
	4 tablespoons (½ stick) butter

Stir the eggs, milk, and salt briskly in a bowl with a fork until well blended. Strain the mixture through a sieve into a shallow bowl in which you can easily dip a slice of bread. Dip both sides of each slice of bread in the batter and place the slices on a piece of waxed paper.

Melt 2 tablespoons of the butter in a skillet big enough to hold 3 slices at once. Fry the bread over medium heat until very lightly browned, turning once. Keep the cooked slices warm in a 250°F oven while frying the other three in the remaining 2 tablespoons of butter. Serve warm sprinkled with confectioners' sugar.

Spiced French Toast   Add ½ teaspoon cinnamon or nutmeg to the batter.

Lemon or Orange French Toast   Add 2 teaspoons grated lemon or orange zest to the batter.

Maple Syrup French Toast   Instead of ¾ cup milk, use ½ cup milk and ¼ cup maple syrup in the batter.

Fruit Syrup French Toast   Reduce the milk in the batter to ½ cup, and add ¼ cup of any fruit syrup.

Buttermilk French Toast   Substitute buttermilk for sweet milk in the batter.

J.B.'s French Toast

(four servings)

This is my favorite French toast recipe. James Beard once told me that they used to serve this in the dining cars on the Santa Fe Railroad. The crumbled-up cornflakes give every bite a crisp crunch that is mighty good.

3 eggs
½ cup milk
½ teaspoon nutmeg
¼ teaspoon salt

2 cups cornflakes
4 tablespoons (½ stick) butter
6 slices dense white bread
6 tablespoons sugar

Stir the eggs, milk, nutmeg, and salt together in a bowl until well blended. Strain the mixture through a sieve into a shallow bowl in which you can dip the bread easily (a soup bowl works well).

Crumble the cornflakes slightly (to make each flake about half its original size) and spread them on a piece of waxed paper.

Dip (don't soak) both sides of each slice of bread into the milk batter. Then press each slice of bread on both sides into the cornflakes to coat the bread well.

Melt 2 tablespoons butter in a 12-inch skillet over medium heat and fry 3 slices of the bread until golden on each side. When done, sprinkle about 1 tablespoon sugar on top of each slice and keep warm in a 250°F oven while you fry the other 3 slices in the remaining 2 tablespoons butter. Serve hot.

BREAKFAST SANDWICHES

Children of all ages love sandwiches, so why not have them for breakfast. Here are some sandwiches that use breakfast ingredients.

Fig and Ham on Rye Bread

For 2 sandwiches, butter 2 slices of bread to the edges. Trim the blossom end and stem from 5 ripe green figs (the Adriatic variety is delicious) and slice each one into 3 slices. Divide the slices of fig between 2 unbuttered slices of bread. Place a very thin slice of ham over each and cover with the buttered bread. Gently press down on each sandwich. Cut in half and serve.

Sausage and Melted Cheese Sandwiches

For 4 open-face sandwiches, slice 1/4 pound cooked sausage links lengthwise and place in a single layer over 4 slices whole wheat bread. Sprinkle 1 1/2 cups grated Cheddar cheese over the sausage. Put the sandwiches under the broiler (watch carefully) and broil until the cheese melts and bubbles.

Walnut Butter Sandwiches

For 2 sandwiches, mix 4 tablespoons room-temperature butter, 2/3 cup ground walnuts, and 1/3 cup golden raisins together in a small bowl, briskly stirring until the mixture has blended. Trim the crusts from 4 slices white bread. Spread the mixture over 2 slices and cover with the other 2 slices. Cut the sandwiches in half and serve with melon.

Date and Breakfast Cheese Sandwiches

For 2 sandwiches, stir together 2/3 cup chopped, pitted dates and 1/3 cup Breakfast Cheese (see page 286) or soft cream cheese until blended. Spread equal amounts on 2 slices of raisin bread and cover with another 2 slices. Cut the sandwiches in half and serve with a few walnut halves on the side.

Strawberry Sandwiches

To make 4 delicious summer Sunday breakfast sandwiches, first wash and hull 4 cups (about 2 baskets) fresh strawberries. Slice half of them, mash the other half, and add sugar to taste to both batches. Combine the sliced and mashed berries, reserving enough slices to garnish the tops of the sandwiches. Whip 1 cup heavy cream and sweeten with 3 tablespoons confectioners' sugar. On each plate, put a slice of good fresh white bread trimmed of its crust (feed the crusts to the birds). Spread the strawberries evenly over each slice, cover with another slice, and spread the whipped cream neatly over the top and sides. Garnish each sandwich with a few strawberry slices and serve at once. (You may prepare the fruit, cream, and bread in advance, and assemble the sandwiches just before serving.) This is not a pick-up sandwich — eat with a knife and fork.

Mexican Breakfast Sandwich

Spread a slice of Mexican Bread (see page 16) with Breakfast Cheese (see page 286) and cover with a layer of fresh cilantro leaves. Top with another slice of Mexican Bread. Melt 2 tablespoons butter over medium-low heat in a skillet, put the sandwich in the pan, and cook, pressing down on the sandwich several times with a spatula. Turn the sandwich over when the bottom is golden, add a little more butter to the skillet if necessary, and cook until golden. Serve with fresh spears of pineapple.

Ham and Farm Cheese Butter-Fried Sandwiches

(two sandwiches)

Here nourishing breakfast ingredients are brought together in a simple form that appeals especially to children.

4 slices fresh whole wheat or
   white bread
About 3 ounces soft cream cheese
   (many markets carry fresh cream
   cheese, which is much better
   than the foil-wrapped variety)

4 thin slices ham
4 tablespoons (½ stick) butter

Lay the 4 slices of bread on a surface and spread each slice on one side with a rounded tablespoon of cream cheese. Place 2 ham slices on top of 2 of the slices and cover with the remaining slices of bread.

Melt the butter over medium-low heat. Place the sandwiches in the pan and fry gently until the bottom is golden, pressing down on each sandwich occasionally with a spatula—this will help to melt the cheese. Turn and fry the other side. Serve warm.

Quick Breads

Cream Biscuits
Oatmeal Biscuits
Buttermilk Barley Biscuits
White Cornbread with Fresh Sage
Custard-Filled Cornbread
Scones
    Brown, Dried Fruit Cream,
    Oatmeal Raisin
Bannocks
    Cheese
Raw Apple Muffins
Bran Muffins
Banana Bran Muffins
Boston Brown Bread Muffins
Chewy Brown Sugar Muffins
Peerless Cornbread Muffins
Cranberry Orange Muffins
Fig Muffins
Bridge Creek Fresh Ginger Muffins
Lemon Yogurt Muffins
Last Word in Nutmeg Muffins
Irish Oatmeal Muffins
Orange Walnut Muffins
Persimmon Muffins
Cinnamon Butter Puffs
Sunday Loaf
Blueberry Cranberry Bread
Date Nut Bread
    Fig Nut, Prune
Dried Fruit Bread
Christmas Bread
Oatmeal Popovers

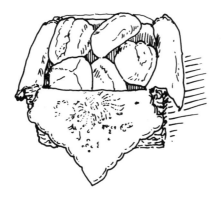

Breakfast quick breads, warm from the oven, puffy and delicious, will gladden the heart. As Marion Harland, once a leading American cook, wrote in 1903, the appearance of hot quick breads on the breakfast board "is a means of breakfast grace not to be underrated by the wise housewife."

Breads leavened with baking powder or baking soda are called quick breads because they are much faster to prepare than breads made with yeast. In our short history, American cooks have invented a marvelous and unique bounty of quick breads. In this chapter you'll find some reinterpretations of traditional favorites, but most are strikingly different recipes with new flavors that you will encounter nowhere else.

It is the easiest thing in the world to have muffins or slices of a quick bread loaf for breakfast. You don't need an electric anything to make them, and the dry ingredients and wet ingredients can be prepared (separately) the night before. In the morning all you will need to do is mix them together, and your biscuits, muffins, or bread can be baking while you're in the shower.

The ideal texture for most quick breads is usually described as pebbly—coarser and more crumbly than the fine, even texture of cake, but still tender. To achieve this, do not overbeat: just mix the wet and dry ingredients together until no floury streaks are showing.

Muffins served hot, straight from the oven, are perfection. Quick breads baked in loaves should rest a while before slicing, but they are nice served warm. Carefully wrap any leftovers and freeze; they keep well. You can freshen thawed-out or slightly stale muffins by dipping them rapidly in cold milk (or water) and then reheating them in the oven.

One word of caution: baking powder gradually loses its strength. If your muffins are flat, it may be because the baking powder is stale, not because you have lost your touch. Always buy the smallest-size can of baking powder, and if you haven't used it up, get rid of it after four or five months and get a new one. Ignore the expiration date on the can: it is always far too optimistic.

Cream Biscuits

(one dozen biscuits)

These biscuits are superior, and no student ever failed to make good ones in James Beard's cooking classes. They are better than most baking powder biscuits, and they are so ridiculously simple, you don't have to be awake to make them. They should be in your permanent recipe file.

2 cups all-purpose flour
1 teaspoon salt
1 tablespoon baking powder
2 teaspoons sugar

1 to 1½ cups heavy cream
⅓ cup (5⅓ tablespoons) butter, melted

Preheat the oven to 425°F. Use an ungreased baking sheet.

Combine the flour, salt, baking powder, and sugar in a mixing bowl. Stir the dry ingredients with a fork to blend and lighten. Slowly add 1 cup of the cream to the mixture, stirring constantly. Gather the dough together; when it holds together and feels tender, it is ready to knead. If the dough seems shaggy and pieces are dry and falling away, then slowly add enough additional cream to make the dough hold together.

Place the dough on a lightly floured board and knead for 1 minute. Pat the dough into a square that is about 1/2 inch thick. Cut into 12 squares and dip each into the melted butter so all sides are coated. Place the biscuits 2 inches apart on the baking sheet. Bake for about 15 minutes, or until the biscuits are lightly browned. Serve hot.

Oatmeal Biscuits

(one dozen biscuits)

These biscuits are not too rich—just oats and buttermilk to give a plain, made-on-the-farm taste.

1/2 cup rolled oats
1 3/4 cups all-purpose flour
1/2 teaspoon salt
1 teaspoon baking powder

1/2 teaspoon baking soda
4 tablespoons (1/2 stick) butter, chilled
3/4 cup buttermilk

Preheat the oven to 425°F. Grease a baking sheet.

Combine the oats, flour, salt, baking powder, and baking soda in a mixing bowl. Stir and toss to mix and blend all the dry ingredients.

Cut the cold butter into pieces and add to the flour mixture. Using your fingers or a pastry cutter, cut or rub the butter into the flour until the mixture is in coarse, irregular bits. Add the buttermilk and stir the mixture with a fork until the rough mass somewhat holds together.

Gather the dough up and place on a lightly floured board. Knead about 10 times, pushing some of the pieces into the ball (this is a rather dry dough). Pat or roll into a 1/2-inch thickness. Cut into 2-inch rounds and place 1 inch apart on the baking sheet.

Bake 12 to 15 minutes, or until lightly browned. Serve hot.

Buttermilk Barley Biscuits

(thirty biscuits)

These rather flat biscuits (they will be only 3/8 inch high) are very tasty spread with cream cheese and jam. The barley lends a homey taste. Eat them warm and freeze whatever is left over.

1¼ cups barley flour
  (available in health food stores)
1¼ cups all-purpose flour
2 teaspoons sugar
1½ teaspoons baking powder
½ teaspoon baking soda
1 teaspoon salt
1 cup buttermilk
¼ cup (½ stick) butter, melted

Preheat the oven to 425°F. Grease a baking sheet.

Put the flours, sugar, baking powder, baking soda, and salt in a mixing bowl. Stir with a fork to mix well. Stir in the buttermilk and beat briskly until mixed and smooth. Add the melted butter and blend well.

Dust a board with flour and turn the dough onto the board. Pat the dough into a piece about ¼ inch thick. Use a 2- or 2½-inch cutter to cut out the biscuits. Prick each biscuit 2 or 3 times on top with the tines of a fork. Place the biscuits a little apart (although these won't spread during baking) on the baking sheet. Bake for 10 to 15 minutes, or until lightly golden. Serve warm.

White Cornbread with Fresh Sage

(one 8-inch square cornbread)

Cornbread has an affinity for sage. Bits of crisp bacon incorporated into the batter can also produce delicious results.

1/4 cup water
1 tablespoon finely chopped
   fresh sage (or, if not available,
   2 teaspoons crumbled
   dried sage)
1 cup all-purpose flour
1 cup white cornmeal
1/2 teaspoon baking soda

1 1/2 teaspoons baking powder
1/2 teaspoon salt
3/4 cup buttermilk
1 egg
1/4 cup (4 tablespoons) vegetable
   shortening, melted
Optional: 1/3 cup crumbled crisp,
   pan-fried bacon

Preheat the oven to 425°F. Grease the square pan.

In a small saucepan, bring 1/4 cup water to a boil, remove from the heat, and stir in the sage. Set aside while you mix the dry ingredients to let the sage infuse the water with flavor.

Combine the flour, cornmeal, baking soda, baking powder, and salt in a mixing bowl. Stir with a fork to mix well. In a small separate bowl, combine the buttermilk, egg, shortening, and the sage and sage-flavored water. Add to the dry mixture with the bacon, if you are using it, and stir only to blend barely.

Spread evenly in the greased pan. Bake about 20 minutes, or until a straw comes out clean when inserted into the center. Remove from the oven and serve hot with butter.

Custard-Filled Cornbread

(eight servings)

This recipe is magic. When the cornbread is done, a creamy, barely set custard will have formed inside, and everyone will try to figure out how you got it there. Jane Salfass Freimann rediscovered this recipe, which was popular in the thirties; for instance, it appeared in Marjorie Kinnan Rawlings' *Cross Creek Country* in a much sweeter version.

2 eggs	1 cup all-purpose flour
3 tablespoons butter, melted	3/4 cup yellow cornmeal
3 tablespoons sugar	1 teaspoon baking powder
1/2 teaspoon salt	1/2 teaspoon baking soda
2 cups milk	1 cup heavy cream
1 1/2 tablespoons white vinegar	

Preheat the oven to 350°F. Butter an 8-inch-square baking dish or pan that is about 2 inches deep. Put the buttered dish or pan in the oven and let it get hot while you mix the batter.

Put the eggs in a mixing bowl and add the melted butter. Beat until the mixture is well blended. Add the sugar, salt, milk, and vinegar and beat well. Sift into a bowl or stir together in a bowl the flour, cornmeal, baking powder, and baking soda and add to the egg mixture. Mix just until the batter is smooth and no lumps appear.

Pour the batter into the heated dish, then pour the cream into the center of the batter—*don't stir*. Bake for 1 hour, or until lightly browned. Serve warm.

BREAKFAST TABLE CIVILITY AND DEPORTMENT

1. Clean up before you come to the breakfast table: wash your face and comb your hair.
2. You don't have to get dressed.
3. Clean fingernails, please.
4. Reading the newspaper at the table is permissable, but a pleasant word or salutation must be spoken to all present.
5. Sit up straight and try to be cheerful.
6. Talk to one another politely; talk and listen in turn.
7. Because everyone is defenseless at breakfast, there should be no contentiousness or crossness.
8. Don't ever mention food dislikes or criticize the food.
9. Don't lick your fingers or stuff your mouth with food.
10. Don't play with your food.
11. Don't talk with your mouth full.
12. Butter your bread one part at a time; don't put your uneaten pieces back in the bread basket.
13. And don't answer questions in a saucy manner.
14. Remember, guests always receive the choicest portions.

M.C.

SCONES

Scones have always been served with afternoon tea, but now they are in vogue on the breakfast table. The ones in this book are all oven-baked scones (there are also drop scones, made like pancakes from a thin batter, and griddle scones, made like oven scones but baked on a griddle). I like scones to be crisp and brown on the top and rather dense on the inside, with a nudge of richness from the butter in them or on them. Scones are delicious when served warm, split and buttered and spread with jam.

Brown Scones

(about one dozen scones)

1½ cups all-purpose flour
½ cup bran
2 teaspoons baking powder
½ teaspoon salt
3 tablespoons sugar
4 tablespoons (½ stick) butter, chilled

1 egg
½ cup milk

Glaze
2 tablespoons milk
2 tablespoons dark brown sugar

Preheat the oven to 450°F. Use an ungreased baking sheet.

Combine the flour, bran, baking powder, salt, and sugar in a bowl and mix well. Cut the butter into bits and add to the flour mixture. Rub the butter into the flour, using your fingertips or a pastry blender, until the mixture resembles coarse bread crumbs. In another bowl, beat the egg lightly, add the milk, and mix until well blended. Stir the milk mixture into the flour mixture, and stir only until just blended.

Lightly dust a board with flour and turn the dough onto the board. Knead about 12 times. Pat into a circle about ½ inch thick. Make the glaze by blending the milk and brown sugar until smooth. Brush this over the dough and cut the dough into 12 wedges. Place the wedges on a baking sheet so that there is a ½-inch space between them.

Bake for 10 to 12 minutes, or until the tops are golden. Serve hot.

Dried Fruit Cream Scones

(one dozen scones)

2 cups all-purpose flour	¼ cup golden raisins
1 tablespoon baking powder	1¼ cups heavy cream
½ teaspoon salt	
¼ cup sugar	*Glaze*
½ cup chopped dried fruit	3 tablespoons butter, melted
(apricots, prunes, or figs)	2 tablespoons sugar

Preheat the oven to 425°F. Use an ungreased baking sheet.

Combine the flour, baking powder, salt, and sugar in a bowl, stirring with a fork to mix well. Add the dried fruit and raisins. Still using a fork, stir in the cream and mix until the dough holds together in a rough mass (the dough will be quite sticky).

Lightly flour a board and transfer the dough to it. Knead the dough 8 or 9 times. Pat into a circle about 10 inches round. For the glaze, spread the butter over the top and side of the circle of dough and sprinkle the sugar on top. Cut the circle into 12 wedges and place each piece on the baking sheet, allowing about an inch between pieces.

Bake for about 15 minutes, or until golden brown.

Oatmeal Raisin Scones

(eighteen scones)

These are super with Caramel Oatmeal Topping (see page 280). Before you cut the dough into wedges, sprinkle ½ cup topping evenly over it, and press firmly into the dough.

4 cups all-purpose flour
⅓ cup sugar
1¾ teaspoons baking powder
1 teaspoon baking soda
1 teaspoon salt

½ pound (2 sticks) butter, chilled
3 cups rolled oats
1 cup raisins
2 cups buttermilk

Preheat the oven to 375°F.

Mix together the flour, sugar, baking powder, baking soda, and salt in a large bowl. Cut the cold butter into small pieces and add to the flour mixture. Use either your fingers or a pastry cutter to rub or cut the butter into the flour mixture until it resembles coarse crumbs. Add the oats and raisins, tossing or stirring with a fork to distribute evenly. Add the buttermilk and stir with a fork until you can gather the dough into a rough ball.

Sprinkle a board with flour and put the dough on it. Knead 6 or 7 times. Divide the dough into 3 equal parts. Pat each part into a circle about ½ inch thick. Cut each circle into 10 wedges. Put the wedges on ungreased baking sheets ½ inch apart. Bake for about 25 minutes, or until the scones are lightly brown. Serve warm.

Bannocks

(eight bannocks)

Bannocks originated in Scotland and northern England centuries ago. Also known as oatcakes, they were made with either barley or oats and cooked on a griddle. Bannocks are the quickest of quick breads, and with little nubbins of oats throughout, they have an appealing taste.

1 cup rolled oats
1 cup oat flour
  (available in health food stores)
¼ teaspoon salt

4 tablespoons (½ stick) butter, chilled
½ cup water

Preheat the oven to 400°F. Grease a baking sheet.

Put the oats, flour, and salt in a mixing bowl and stir with a fork to blend. Cut the cold butter into small pieces and add to the flour mixture. Rub the butter and flour together until coarse bits form. Stir in the water and mix. Gather the rough dough together and place on a board that has been lightly dusted with oat flour. Knead the dough about 6 times. Divide the dough in half and pat each half into a circle about ¼ inch thick. Cut each circle into 4 wedges. Place the wedges on the greased baking sheet ½ inch apart. Bake about 20 minutes, or until lightly colored.

Cheese Bannocks   Add 1 cup grated Cheddar cheese to the mixture after rubbing in the butter. Proceed as directed above.

Raw Apple Muffins

(sixteen muffins)

These muffins are different because they are not light and airy; instead, they are dense with fruit and raisins and nuts. You'll find them particularly moist and full of spicy good flavor.

4 cups diced apple (peeled or unpeeled)	2 teaspoons baking soda
1 cup sugar	2 teaspoons cinnamon
2 eggs, beaten lightly	1 teaspoon salt
½ cup oil (corn oil is very good)	1 cup raisins
2 teaspoons vanilla extract	1 cup broken walnuts (leave in large pieces)
2 cups all-purpose flour	

Preheat the oven to 325°F. Grease 16 muffin tins.

Put 3 mixing bowls on the counter. Mix the apples and sugar in one bowl and set aside. Put the eggs, oil, and vanilla in the second bowl and stir to blend well. In the third bowl, put the flour, baking soda, cinnamon, and salt, and stir the mixture with a fork until blended.

Stir the egg mixture into the apples and sugar, and mix thoroughly. Sprinkle the flour mixture over the apple mixture and mix well. (I use my hands because this is a stiff batter.) Sprinkle the raisins and walnuts over the batter and mix until they are evenly distributed. Spoon into the muffin tins.

Bake for about 25 minutes, or until a straw comes out clean when inserted into the center of a muffin. Serve warm.

Bran Muffins

(eighteen muffins)

This is a perfect recipe for a child to make: just measure, stir, and spoon into muffin tins. These bran muffins are moist and lightly sweetened, with a nice balance of flavor—quite a good contrast to some of the sticky, cloyingly sweet bran muffins that are supposed to be good for you.

2½ cups bran	⅔ cup buttermilk
1⅓ cups whole wheat flour	⅓ cup vegetable oil
2½ teaspoons baking soda	⅓ cup dark molasses
½ teaspoon salt	¼ cup honey
2 eggs	1 cup raisins

Preheat the oven to 425°F. Grease the muffin tins.

Put the bran, flour, baking soda, and salt in a bowl and stir to blend. Add the eggs, buttermilk, oil, molasses, and honey to the bran mixture and beat until blended. Stir in the raisins.

Fill the muffin tins two-thirds full. Bake for about 12 to 15 minutes, or until the muffins have shrunk from the sides of the pan. Serve warm.

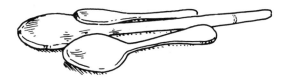

Banana Bran Muffins

(two dozen muffins)

These are head and shoulders above the dense, serious, prescription-type bran muffins that are eaten because they are good for you; and the cake flour makes them particularly light. They are moist, tender, and nicely flavored with banana.

12 tablespoons (1½ sticks) butter, room temperature	1½ cups bran
	¾ teaspoon salt
⅔ cup sugar	1½ teaspoons baking soda
4 medium-size *ripe* bananas (to make 2½ to 3 cups purée)	Optional: 1 cup chopped walnuts; 1 tablespoon grated orange zest;
3 eggs	¾ cup granola
2 cups cake flour	

Preheat the oven to 375°F. Grease the muffin pans.

Put the butter in a mixing bowl and beat until creamy. Add the sugar and blend well. Stir in the banana purée and eggs, and beat until the batter is light and smooth.

Sift the flour, bran, salt, and baking soda together (I sift onto a sheet of waxed paper), then add the flour mixture to the batter and mix well. Add any or all of the optional ingredients at this point. Spoon the batter into muffin pans, almost filling them. Bake 15 to 20 minutes. Serve warm.

Serve with fruit or a tangy yogurt, like lemon.

Boston Brown Bread Muffins

(one dozen muffins)

Boston Brown Bread Muffins have all the virtues of classic steamed brown bread but are much quicker to make.

½ cup rye flour
½ cup yellow cornmeal
½ cup whole wheat flour
¾ teaspoon salt
1½ teaspoons baking soda
1 egg

⅓ cup molasses
⅓ cup firmly packed dark brown
  sugar
⅓ cup vegetable oil
1 cup buttermilk
1 cup golden raisins

Preheat the oven to 400°F. Grease the muffin tins.

Mix together with a fork the rye flour, cornmeal, whole wheat flour, salt, and baking soda in a large bowl until blended. In a small bowl combine the egg, molasses, brown sugar, oil, and buttermilk. Stir or beat to blend well. Stir the egg mixture into the flour mixture and mix well. Add the raisins and stir to mix.

Fill the muffin tins about one-half to two-thirds full. Bake for 15 minutes, or until a straw comes out clean when inserted into the center of a muffin. Don't overbake! Serve hot.

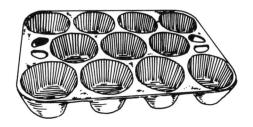

Chewy Brown Sugar Muffins

(eighteen muffins)

There is nothing flimsy about these muffins—the distinct tastes of brown sugar and oats come through, with a hint of maple. Eat them with crisp bacon, or maybe even an egg.

1 cup heavy cream
1 cup pancake syrup*
2 eggs
¾ cup whole wheat flour
¾ cup all-purpose flour
½ cup firmly packed dark brown
  sugar

¾ teaspoon salt
2 teaspoons baking powder
1 teaspoon baking soda
1½ cups rolled oats
Optional: 1 cup broken walnut
  pieces

*Do not substitute all maple syrup. If you wish to, you may use ½ cup maple syrup and ½ cup dark corn syrup in place of the pancake syrup.

Preheat the oven to 350°F. Grease the muffin tins.

In a large mixing bowl, combine the cream, syrup, eggs, flours, sugar, salt, baking powder, baking soda, and oats and beat with a whisk (this is so easy that you don't need an electric anything to make these). If adding the walnuts, stir them in now.

Fill the muffin tins three-quarters full. Bake about 20 minutes, or until a straw comes out clean when inserted into the center.

Peerless Cornbread Muffins

(one dozen muffins)

Tender-textured yellow muffins—the only bread I know that isn't improved by being buttered. Do I need to remind you that honey is pleasing with cornbread?

1 egg, room temperature
½ cup (1 stick) butter, melted
¼ cup vegetable oil
1 cup milk, warmed
1 cup cake flour

⅔ cup yellow cornmeal
1 tablespoon baking powder
½ teaspoon salt
1 tablespoon sugar

Preheat the oven to 400°F. Grease the muffin tins.

Beat or whisk the egg, melted butter, and oil in a mixing bowl until well blended. Stir in the warm milk. Combine the cake flour, cornmeal, baking powder, salt, and sugar in another bowl and stir with a fork until well mixed. Add the dry ingredients to the egg mixture and stir until blended. This is a light, medium-thick batter.

Spoon the batter into the muffin tins so each cup is three-quarters full. Bake for 15 to 20 minutes, or until the edges of the muffins are slightly golden and a straw comes out clean when inserted into the center. Remove from tins and cool a little on racks, or simply serve in a basket, hot from the oven.

Cranberry Orange Muffins

(about three dozen tiny muffins)

These small, moist, bite-size muffins are best served slightly warm, so if you make them ahead, reheat them on a baking sheet in a hot oven for a few minutes before serving and then toss again in cinnamon sugar. At Thanksgiving time, you might want to buy a few extra bags of cranberries and store them in the freezer, so you can make cranberry muffins all year long. These should be made in small cupcake pans—those with a top diameter of 1 3/4 inches.

1 1/2 cups all-purpose flour
1 teaspoon baking soda
1/2 teaspoon baking powder
1/4 teaspoon salt

1/4 cup sugar
1 egg
1/2 cup buttermilk
1/3 cup (5 1/3 tablespoons) butter, melted

1/4 cup orange marmalade
1/2 cup finely chopped fresh cranberries

Cinnamon Sugar
2/3 cup sugar
2 teaspoons cinnamon

Preheat the oven to 375°F. Butter small cupcake pans (1 3/4 inch top diameter, and about 3/4 inch deep). If you don't have enough muffin tins, bake the muffins in relays, like cookies.

In a small mixing bowl, stir and toss together the flour, baking soda, baking powder, and salt. In another, larger bowl, place the sugar, egg, buttermilk, melted butter, marmalade, and cranberries, and beat until completely blended. Add the combined dry ingredients and beat just until blended.

Spoon the batter into the prepared muffin tins, filling each cup almost to the top. Bake for 12 to 15 minutes, or until a toothpick or straw inserted into the center of a muffin comes out clean.

While the muffins bake, stir the sugar and cinnamon together in a pie plate or shallow dish. As soon as the muffins are done, immediately remove them from the pans and roll them gently, 4 or 5 at a time, in the sugar mixture. Transfer them to a rack until ready to serve. Once muffins are completely cool, wrap airtight and freeze any you won't use immediately.

Fig Muffins

(eighteen muffins)

Figs are often overlooked in baking, but they are high on the list of fruits that are good for you.

1/4 cup vegetable shortening
1/3 cup sugar
1 egg, lightly beaten
1/2 cup milk
2 cups coarsely chopped fresh figs
  (either Mission or Adriatic);
  or 1 1/2 cups coarsely chopped
  dried Calimyrna figs

1 cup all-purpose flour
1/2 cup whole wheat flour
1/2 teaspoon salt
2 teaspoons baking powder

Preheat the oven to 375°F. Grease the muffin tins.

Combine the shortening and sugar and mix until smooth and blended. Add the egg and milk and beat well. Add the figs and mix thoroughly.

Put the flours, salt, and baking powder in a bowl and stir with a fork just enough to mix. Add to the fig mixture and stir only until no floury streaks show — don't overmix.

Spoon the batter into the muffin tins, filling two-thirds full. Bake about 20 minutes, or until a straw comes out clean when inserted into the center of a muffin. Remove muffins from tins to cool.

Bridge Creek Fresh Ginger Muffins

(sixteen muffins)

These muffins have an abundance of fresh ginger and lemon zest. Every time I make them I am overcome by how good they are.

A 2-ounce piece unpeeled
   gingerroot
3/4 cup plus 3 tablespoons sugar
2 tablespoons lemon zest (from 2
   lemons), with some white pith
8 tablespoons (1 stick) butter,
   room temperature

2 eggs
1 cup buttermilk
2 cups all-purpose flour
1/2 teaspoon salt
3/4 teaspoon baking soda

Preheat the oven to 375°F. Grease the muffin tins.

Cut the *unpeeled* ginger into large chunks. If you have a food processor, process the ginger until it is in tiny pieces; or hand chop into fine pieces. (You should have 1/4 cup. It is better to have too much ginger than too little.) Put the ginger and 1/4 cup sugar in a small skillet or pan and cook over medium heat until the sugar has melted and the mixture is hot. Don't walk away from the pan — this cooking takes only a couple of minutes. Remove from the stove and let the ginger mixture cool.

Put the lemon zest and 3 tablespoons sugar in the food processor and process until the lemon peel is in small bits; or chop the lemon zest and pith by hand and then add the sugar. Add the lemon mixture to the ginger mixture. Stir and set aside.

Put the butter in a mixing bowl and beat a second or two, add the remaining 1/2 cup sugar, and beat until smooth. Add the eggs and beat well. Add the buttermilk and mix until blended. Add the flour, salt, and baking soda. Beat until smooth. Add the ginger-lemon mixture and mix well.

Spoon the batter into the muffin tins so that each cup is three-quarters full. Bake 15 to 20 minutes. Serve warm.

Lemon Yogurt Muffins

(about one dozen muffins)

These yellow muffins with brown pebbly tops are fine-textured and not too sweet. They go especially well with hot tea. Lemon syrup drizzled over after baking makes them extra moist.

2 cups all-purpose flour
1 teaspoon baking powder
1 teaspoon baking soda
1/4 teaspoon salt
1/4 cup sugar
2 tablespoons honey
2 eggs
1 1/4 cups plain yogurt

1/4 cup (1/2 stick) butter, melted
1 tablespoon grated lemon zest

Lemon Syrup
1/3 cup lemon juice
1/3 cup sugar
3 tablespoons water

Preheat the oven to 375°F and butter the muffin tins.

In a small mixing bowl, stir and toss together the flour, baking powder, baking soda, and salt. In another, larger bowl, combine the sugar, honey, eggs, yogurt, melted butter, and lemon zest and beat until thoroughly mixed. Add the combined dry ingredients and beat just until blended.

Spoon the batter into the prepared muffin tins, filling each cup about two-thirds full. These should bake for about 15 minutes, or until the tops are delicately browned and a toothpick or straw inserted into the center of a muffin comes out clean.

While the muffins bake, prepare the syrup. Combine the lemon juice, sugar, and water in a small saucepan. Bring to a boil, boil for 1 minute, then set aside.

When the muffins are done, remove the pan from the oven and

gently poke the top of each muffin two or three times with a fork. Drizzle about 2 teaspoons of the syrup over each hot muffin, letting it run over the top and around the edge. Let cool in the pans for a few minutes, then remove and serve warm.

Last Word in Nutmeg Muffins

(one dozen muffins)

Fragrant, creamy-crumbed nutmeg muffins, the best of their kind, but you must grate one and a half whole little nutmegs to make these perfect creations. Although whole nutmegs feel like rocks, they are rather soft and easy to grate. The flavor of freshly grated nutmeg is incomparable. These muffins taste good with fruit, or butter, or all by themselves.

2 cups all-purpose flour	1 egg
¾ cup sugar	¾ cup heavy cream
1 tablespoon baking powder	¾ cup milk
1½ whole nutmegs, grated	5 tablespoons butter, melted
½ teaspoon salt	

Preheat the oven to 400°F. Grease the muffin tins.

Stir together with a fork the flour, sugar, baking powder, nutmeg, and salt in a medium-size bowl, thoroughly combining the ingredients. Beat the egg well in a small bowl, then stir in the cream, milk, and butter and blend well. Add the cream mixture to the flour mixture and stir only until there are no streaks of flour. Don't overmix.

Spoon batter two-thirds full into each muffin cup. Bake for about 20 minutes, or until the rounded tops are lightly golden. Remove muffins from the pan, and serve warm. Or cool on a rack and store or freeze for later use; warm before serving.

Irish Oatmeal Muffins

(two dozen muffins)

The Irish often cook their oatmeal all night long for a rich and creamy effect. These muffins take on that same flavor from overnight soaking in buttermilk. Try spreading a little Whipped Maple Syrup (see page 281) on them.

2 cups buttermilk	1⅔ cups whole wheat flour
1 cup rolled oats	1 teaspoon baking soda
2 eggs	1 teaspoon salt
¾ cup dark brown sugar	2 tablespoons vegetable oil

Combine the buttermilk and the oats at least 6 hours (preferably overnight) before mixing and baking the muffins. Stir well, cover, and let rest in the refrigerator.

Preheat the oven to 400°F. Grease the muffin tins.

Put the eggs in a mixing bowl and beat just until yolk and white are blended. Add the sugar and beat until smooth and well blended. Add the buttermilk-oatmeal mixture. Add the flour, baking soda, salt, and oil. Beat until the batter is well mixed.

Fill the muffin tins three-quarters full of batter. They usually bake about 20 minutes, but start testing for doneness after 15 minutes. Either remove the muffins from the tins and cool on racks or serve hot from the pan.

Orange Walnut Muffins

(sixteen muffins)

It is amazing how the flavor of two oranges can so completely permeate sixteen muffins that they taste of the essence of orange. Chopping the zest and the flesh of the orange is done in a flash with the food processor, although it is also easy to do this little bit of chopping by hand.

2 large oranges	2 cups all-purpose flour
(not too many seeds)	2 teaspoons baking powder
2 eggs	1/2 teaspoon baking soda
1/2 cup sugar	1/2 teaspoon salt
1/2 cup (1 stick) butter, melted	1/2 cup chopped walnuts

Preheat the oven to 400°F. Grease the muffin tins.

Using a small paring knife or grater, remove the zest from the orange (the zest is the colored skin without the bitter white pith beneath). Trim off the pith and the white membrane and discard, leaving just the orange flesh. Chop the oranges fine along with the zest (by hand or in a food processor); you should have about 1 cup. Set aside into a small bowl.

Put the eggs in a large bowl and lightly whisk to blend. Add the sugar and butter and stir well. Combine the flour, baking powder, baking soda, and salt in another bowl and stir to blend. Then add the orange and the flour mixture to the egg mixture and stir until blended. Stir in the walnuts.

Fill the muffin tins one-half to two-thirds full. Bake for about 15 minutes, or until a straw comes out clean when inserted into the center of a muffin. Serve hot.

Persimmon Muffins

(eighteen muffins)

This recipe is adapted from my favorite steamed persimmon pudding, which is the only cakelike recipe I know using persimmons that works. Persimmons have a short season, but peeled and puréed they freeze well.

1 cup puréed persimmons	½ teaspoon salt
1 teaspoon baking soda	1 teaspoon cinnamon
12 tablespoons (1½ sticks) butter, room temperature	1 teaspoon vanilla extract
1¼ cups sugar	2 teaspoons lemon juice
2 eggs	Optional: 2 tablespoons bourbon
1⅓ cups all-purpose flour	1 cup walnut pieces
	¾ cup currants

Preheat the oven to 325°F. Grease the muffin tins.

Put the puréed persimmons into a small bowl and stir in the baking soda. Set aside.

Put the butter in a mixing bowl and beat, slowly adding the sugar, until the mixture is creamy and smooth. Add the eggs and beat well. Add the flour, salt, and cinnamon along with the persimmon mixture and beat until well blended. Add the vanilla, lemon juice, and optional bourbon. Stir in the walnuts and currants.

Fill each muffin cup three-quarters full. Bake for 45 minutes, or until a straw comes out clean when inserted into the center of a muffin. Remove from the muffin pans and let cool on racks or serve warm.

Cinnamon Butter Puffs

(about one dozen puffs)

Recipes for puffs—really just muffins rolled in spiced sugar (with cinnamon, mace, etc.)—were popular at the beginning of this century. Although not necessarily puffier than most muffins, they give the illusion of cake doughnuts.

⅓ cup shortening
½ cup sugar (less if desired)
1 egg
1½ cups all-purpose flour
1½ teaspoons baking powder
½ teaspoon salt
¼ teaspoon nutmeg
½ cup milk

Topping
½ cup (1 stick) butter, melted
½ cup sugar combined with
   1 teaspoon cinnamon

Preheat the oven to 350°F. Grease the muffin tins.

Put the shortening, sugar, and egg in a mixing bowl. Beat well. Mix together the flour, baking powder, salt, and nutmeg and add to the first mixture. Pour in the milk and beat until blended and smooth.

Fill the muffin tins about two-thirds full. Bake about 20 minutes, or until lightly golden.

For the topping, have the melted butter ready in a bowl that is just large enough to hold one puff. Have a shallow bowl ready nearby with the combined sugar and cinnamon. As soon as the puffs are done, remove them from the pan and dip them one by one into the melted butter, and then roll in the cinnamon-sugar mixture.

Sunday Loaf

(one large loaf)

This shiny-topped bread is alive with lots of berry flavor. Slice and freeze any leftover loaf and reheat by the slice in your toaster.

3 cups all-purpose flour
½ cup sugar
4 teaspoons baking powder
1 teaspoon salt
8 tablespoons (1 stick) butter, chilled
2 eggs
½ cup raspberry or strawberry jam or preserves (not jelly)
¾ cup milk

Glaze
2 tablespoons butter
2 tablespoons sugar
2 tablespoons raspberry or strawberry jam

Preheat the oven to 350°F. Grease a 9 × 5 × 3-inch loaf pan.

Combine the flour, sugar, baking powder, and salt in a large mixing bowl. Stir with a fork to mix all the dry ingredients well. Cut the butter into small pieces and drop into the flour mixture. Using your fingers or a pastry cutter, rub or cut the cold butter into the flour until the mixture resembles coarse bread crumbs.

Beat the eggs well in a small bowl, add the jam and milk, and whisk until the mixture is blended smooth. Stir the jam mixture into the flour mixture and stir only until no flour streaks show—the mixture will be lumpy.

Spoon into the loaf pan and bake for about 1 hour and 15 minutes, or until a straw inserted into the center comes out clean. Allow the loaf to remain in the pan for 15 to 20 minutes before turning it onto a rack.

Meanwhile, make the glaze by combining the butter, sugar, and jam in a pan. Stir and bring to a simmer; continue stirring until dissolved and blended. Strain and then spoon the glaze over the loaf after it has cooled on the rack.

Blueberry Cranberry Bread

(one large loaf)

Blueberries and cranberries bring out the best in each other. This bread is nicest when you serve it warm.

1 cup fresh cranberries	1 cup buttermilk
¾ cup granulated sugar	3 cups all-purpose flour
1 cup brown sugar	1 teaspoon baking soda
8 tablespoons (1 stick) butter,	1 teaspoon baking powder
room temperature	1 teaspoon salt
2 eggs	1 cup blueberries

Preheat the oven to 375°F. Grease a 9 × 5 × 3-inch loaf pan.

Put the cranberries and granulated sugar in a small skillet and cook over medium heat, stirring often, until the sugar has dissolved. Remove from heat and set aside to cool.

Put the cup of brown sugar and the butter in a mixing bowl and beat until blended. Add the eggs and beat well. Stir in the buttermilk.

Put the flour, baking soda, baking powder, and salt in a bowl and stir with a fork until well mixed. Add to the butter mixture and beat only until blended. Stir in the cranberry mixture and the blueberries. Spoon the batter into the loaf pan.

Bake for about 1 hour and 10 minutes, or until a straw comes out clean when inserted into the center. Remove from the oven and turn onto a rack to cool a little.

Date Nut Bread

(one medium loaf)

I have one finicky eater in my house, and when he tasted this bread and said it was good I knew I had a winner. Bake it and see.

1 cup pitted and chopped dates	¾ cup boiling water
1 cup coarsely chopped walnuts	2 eggs
1½ teaspoons baking soda	¾ cup sugar
½ teaspoon salt	½ cup whole wheat flour
3 tablespoons vegetable shortening	1 cup all-purpose flour

Preheat the oven to 350°F. Grease an 8½ × 4½ × 3-inch loaf pan.

Put the dates, walnuts, baking soda, salt, and shortening in a bowl. Pour the boiling water over and stir. Let the mixture stand for 15 minutes.

Using a fork, beat the eggs and sugar together in a bowl. Add the flours and stir (this will be too stiff to mix well). Add the date mixture and mix briskly until the batter is well blended. Spoon into the loaf pan and bake for about 1 hour, or until a straw comes out clean when inserted into the center. Remove and cool on a rack.

Fig Nut Bread Substitute 1 cup chopped figs for the dates. Proceed as directed above.

Prune Bread Omit the dates and walnuts. Substitute 1½ cups pitted, chopped prunes. Proceed as directed above.

Dried Fruit Bread

(two medium loaves)

This is a fine holiday bread when a small tasty breakfast is in order. Dried Fruit Bread with a good homemade eggnog is a simple and complete breakfast. My family is fond of this recipe because there is no spice to hide the good natural flavor of the fruits. You may use any dried fruit or fruits you choose; we favor figs, apricots, and raisins.

1 cup dried Calimyrna figs	1 egg
1 cup dried apricots	1 teaspoon grated lemon zest
1 cup golden raisins	2 cups all-purpose flour
1½ cups water	2 teaspoons baking powder
1 cup pitted dates	1 teaspoon baking soda
¼ cup shortening	1 teaspoon salt
¾ cup sugar	

Preheat the oven to 350°F. Grease two 8½ × 4½ × 3-inch loaf pans.

Put the figs, apricots, and raisins in a small saucepan and add the water. Partially cover the pan with a lid and simmer for 5 minutes. Drain, reserving ⅔ cup liquid. Cool. Chop the figs, apricots, raisins, and dates.

Put the shortening in a bowl and add the sugar, egg, and lemon zest. Beat until smooth and creamy. Put the flour, baking powder, baking soda, and salt in a bowl and stir with a fork until well mixed. Add all the fruit to the flour mixture, stir in the reserved fruit liquid, and mix until all is blended. Spoon the batter into the loaf pans. Let the pans stand for 15 minutes. Put into the oven and bake for about 45 minutes, or until a straw comes out clean when inserted into the center.

Christmas Bread

(two medium loaves or two dozen muffins)

The citrus zest and fresh spiciness—in combination with an abundance of raisins and currants that have been soaked in almond liqueur—evoke all the tastes of Christmas. I predict that this splendid but easy recipe will become a tradition in your Christmas festivities.

1 cup raisins
½ cup currants
Grated rind with a little white pith of 1 orange
Grated rind with a little white pith of 1 lemon (orange and lemon zest combined should make about ½ cup)
¼ cup almond liqueur (or brandy, rum, or bourbon)
⅓ cup granulated sugar

2 eggs
½ cup vegetable oil
2½ cups all-purpose flour
½ teaspoon salt
1 teaspoon baking soda
1 tablespoon baking powder
1 cup brown sugar
¼ teaspoon ground cloves
1 teaspoon nutmeg (freshly grated, if possible)
1 cup milk

Preheat the oven to 325°F. Grease two 8½ × 4½ × 3-inch loaf pans or muffin tins.

Put the raisins, currants, and grated orange and lemon rind in a small bowl. Pour the liqueur over and add the granulated sugar. Toss the mixture and let macerate for 30 minutes or longer.

Put the eggs and oil in a mixing bowl and whisk until smooth and creamy. Add the flour, salt, baking soda, baking powder, brown sugar, cloves, nutmeg, and milk. Stir vigorously until the mixture is well blended. Stir in the raisins, currants, and orange and lemon rind along with any of the liquid at the bottom of their bowl. Mix well.

Spoon the batter into the loaf pans or muffin tins. Bake the loaves for 1 hour and 15 minutes, or until a wooden skewer comes out clean when inserted into the center. Let the loaves rest 10 minutes in the pans, turn onto racks, and cool before slicing. The bread is best when it is cooled and then rewarmed before serving. If making muffins, bake for about 25 minutes, or until a straw inserted into the center of one comes out clean. The muffins may be turned out onto racks immediately and served hot.

Oatmeal Popovers

(ten popovers)

Popovers are a type of quick bread that rises on egg power alone. The foolproof trick for making high and mighty popovers is to start them in a cold oven. I use some ground oatmeal in this recipe to give the popovers additional texture, and I like to put a rounded teaspoon of tart orange marmalade in the bottom of the custard cups or muffin tins—the combination of oatmeal and orange marmalade is very good.

2 eggs
1 cup milk
1 tablespoon butter, melted
⅓ cup rolled oats, coarsely
  ground in a food processor
  or blender

¾ cup all-purpose flour
½ teaspoon salt
Optional: ½ cup tart orange
  marmalade

Butter the custard cups or muffin tins. Put a rounded teaspoon of marmalade in the bottom of each cup.

Mix the eggs, milk, butter, oatmeal, flour, and salt just until well blended. Half fill the prepared pans with the batter and set them in a cold oven. Turn the heat to 450°F and bake for 15 minutes, then reduce the heat to 350° and bake another 10 to 15 minutes, or just until golden and round. Remove from the pans and serve piping hot.

Cereals

Hot Cereals
  Wheat
  Rice
  Corn
    Bacon Scrapple
    Pumpkin Mush
    Good Grits
  Brown Barley
  Oats and Oatmeal
    Rolled Oats
    Steel-Cut Oats
Cold Cereals
  Granola
  Unsweetened Granola
  Four-Grain Toasted Cereal with
  Bananas and Pecans
  Original Bircher Muesli
  Muesli Ballymaloe

Never think of cereals as being humble – they can be as delicious as caviar, and as healthy as sunshine.

The dried seeds of grassy plants have fed and strengthened us for centuries. Because we don't have beaks like birds and can't chew like horses, man has inventively shaped these grains into many forms: we've milled them, cracked them, puffed them, cooked them and steamed them, and rolled them flat.

HOT CEREALS

All grains can be made into hot cereals. If you're ambling through a health food store, you have an opportunity to have an adventure with some grains you may not have tried – or even heard of – like sorghum, millet, barley, buckwheat, or triticale. There are three basic ways to eat them: raw, with water or milk; slightly cooked by pouring boiling water over them and letting them sit a minute; or as porridge, cooked slowly in simmering water. Read the packaging for cooking instructions – some grains are precooked and need little additional cooking, others, like whole wheat berries, take hours.

There are plenty of ways to prepare and serve hot cereals: you can cook different cereals together for variety; you can serve them with butter, with maple syrup or brown sugar, with applesauce stirred in, with fresh fruit, with raisins and other dried fruits, with nuts, with granola . . .

It seems that most of the world has forgotten that leftover cooked mush—for example, hominy grits or cornmeal mush—is one step away from a delicious fried dish. When the mush is cool, it is put into a buttered loaf pan, covered, and chilled until firm. When ready to fry, the loaf of mush is removed from its pan and cut into ½-inch-thick slices which are fried in hot butter or bacon fat on each side until golden around the edges. Fried mush is good as is, with maple syrup or honey on top, or with eggs and sausage—a fine example of a simple food rising to heights when properly seasoned and cooked.

Wheat

Hulled wheat kernels are called wheat berries and make delicious cereal, but they do take up to three hours to cook. Farina, or cream of wheat, is a ground meal made from refined wheat, and usually enriched or fortified. It is especially good with a little granola stirred in for crunch and flavor. Bulgur is precooked, cracked wheat; it takes only about 15 minutes to cook and makes a nutty-tasting earthy breakfast cereal. It is even better when it is toasted first in the oven to bring out its flavor.

Rice

You might want to try eating rice porridge for breakfast, as they do in China. Try making it with brown rice—it's better for you. Cream of rice is a precooked hot cereal made from granulated white rice, and is usually fortified.

Corn

Both white and yellow cornmeal is available and the two taste identical: choose whichever color you like better—you can make mush with either kind. You can keep cornmeal from lumping by wetting it with cold water before you add it to boiling water.

Dried corn treated with lye to remove the hull and germ is called hominy. It is eaten for breakfast ground up into a coarse meal, called hominy grits, which cooks up into a soothing and satisfying mush. Grits are good with maple syrup or brown sugar, butter, and raisins; or you can jazz them up by serving them with Salsa Verde (see page 284).

Bacon Scrapple

(four servings)

This scrapple will convert scrapple loathers into scrapple addicts. Yellow cornmeal is cooked with a bay leaf and a little bacon fat until it is thick and creamy. Bits of crisp-cooked bacon are added, then the mixture is packed into a loaf pan and chilled overnight. At breakfast time, the loaf is sliced and the slices are fried in a little bacon fat until brown and crisp around the edges. Serve alone with maple syrup or with well-peppered eggs.

½ pound sliced bacon
⅔ cup yellow cornmeal
1 cup cold water
3 cups boiling water

1¼ teaspoons salt
½ teaspoon coarsely ground
  pepper
1 bay leaf, crumbled

Fry the bacon until crisp, pat dry of excess fat on paper towels, and chop into small pieces. Reserve the bacon fat.

Stir the cornmeal into the cold water (always stir cornmeal into cold liquid before adding it to boiling liquid – this keeps the cornmeal from lumping). In a heavy-bottomed saucepan, to the 3 cups boiling water add the salt, pepper, and bay leaf. Stir in the cornmeal and 4 tablespoons bacon fat, lower the heat to medium, and cook, stirring often (as the mixture thickens, be careful not to get too close because the cornmeal will sputter). Cook for about 20 minutes, or until the mixture is no longer runny and thick enough to plop off the spoon.

Remove from the heat and stir in the bacon bits. Oil a medium-size loaf pan and spoon the scrapple into the pan. Let cool, cover, and refrigerate at least 4 hours before pan frying. The mixture must set and become firm.

Cut the loaf into 1/2-inch slices. Heat a skillet over medium heat with some of the bacon fat, and fry each slice until it is brown and crisp around the edges. Serve hot.

Pumpkin Mush

(three cups)

This Pumpkin Mush, adapted from a recipe by Eliza Leslie in her 1852 cookbook, *New Receipts for Cooking,* is, as she says, "an excellent and wholesome breakfast dish." It combines pumpkin purée, yellow cornmeal, and milk and has a slight ginger flavor. Served hot, with a pat of butter and a spoonful of brown sugar, this is *good.*

2 cups milk	1/3 cup cold water
1 cup puréed pumpkin	1/4 teaspoon salt
2/3 cup yellow cornmeal	1 teaspoon ground ginger

Put the milk and pumpkin in a heavy-bottomed saucepan with a lid. Heat, stirring to blend, over medium-low heat.

Put the cornmeal in a small bowl and stir in the cold water (always wet cornmeal with cold water before adding to a hot liquid – this prevents it from getting lumpy). Stir the cornmeal mixture into the milk and pumpkin, and add the salt and ginger. Cook until thickened, stirring every minute or two to keep the mush from burning. (Like all mush, when the mass gets hot it begins to sputter and spurt, so keep the pan partially covered when cooking and remove the pan from the heat to stir to protect yourself from burns.) The mush will be done cooking in only 3 or 4 minutes. Remove from the heat and spoon into bowls. Serve hot. Or serve as fried pumpkin mush, referring to the basic recipe for fried mush on page 82.

Good Grits

(two cups cooked grits)

Many of us Northerners have been awakened late in life to the down-home deliciousness of a bowl of piping hot grits with brown sugar and milk. Grits also make a breakfast pie that is just right for a summer morning.

For variety, try adding ½ cup Grape-Nuts or granola to the cooked grits, or adding 2 tablespoons of yellow cornmeal while cooking.

2 cups water   Optional: butter
Salt to taste
½ cup grits
   (quick-cooking variety)

Bring the water to a boil and add salt. Slowly stir in the grits, and stir for a few seconds more. Turn the heat to medium-low and cover the pan. Cook, stirring once or twice, for 5 minutes. Remove from the heat and stir in a pat of butter, if desired. Serve hot.

Brown Barley

(three cups)

Cooked whole kernel barley has a chewy texture and the compelling taste of field, sun, and rain. The marvels of this grain have escaped me all these years because I always have cooked pearl barley, which is pallid in comparison. Serve yourself a hot bowl of barley with a dot of butter, a sprinkle of brown sugar, and a dash of cream. Make enough to keep and reheat for several days.

3 cups water
Salt to taste
1 cup whole grain barley

Bring the water to a boil and add salt. Stir in the barley, turn the heat to low, and cover the pot. Cook over low heat for about 1 hour to 1 hour and 15 minutes, stirring occasionally and checking for doneness. It should be tender but chewy. Serve hot.

Oats and Oatmeal

In Scotland, where oats are the staple grain, inventive cooks over the centuries have come up with an amazing array of oat dishes. There is porridge, brose (porridge cooked with butter), sowans (fermented oat husks), meal-and-ale (oatmeal cooked up with ale, molasses, and whiskey), hodgils (a kind of oatmeal dumpling), crowdie (raw oatmeal with buttermilk or fresh spring water), to name a few.

Oats make perhaps the best hot cereal because they have more protein than most grains and a high fat content. Porridge made with oatmeal is extremely filling.

Gruel is one oatmeal dish that sounds pitiful and frugal to us, but it was an old-fashioned curative that was supposed to do all kinds of wonderful things for a person. I think it behooves us all to cook up a little gruel once and see how it makes us feel. It is made by pouring 1 cup of cold water over 2 tablespoons of oatmeal. Let stand for 20 minutes, then strain, forcing all the liquid out of the meal and into a pan. Put the pan on the stove and bring to a simmer, adding a bit of butter, honey, or sugar. Sometimes a pinch of nutmeg or a little wine is added.

Rolled Oats

(two servings)

In this country, almost all the oats we eat are rolled oats—steam-treated oats rolled into flakes. You will find regular and quick-cooking kinds in the supermarket. The only difference between the two is the thickness of the oat flake—regular rolled oats are thicker flakes than the quick oats. I prefer the regular kind for its coarser texture.

Try toasting oatmeal before cooking it: spread the oatmeal out on a baking sheet and toast the flakes until they are dark golden. Cook them in the usual way. Toasting the oats gives them a tasty, nutty flavor.

1½ cups boiling water
½ teaspoon salt
⅔ cup rolled oats

Stir the oats into the boiling salted water. If you want creamy oatmeal, cook for about 7 minutes, stirring often. Remove from the heat, cover the pot, and let stand for 5 more minutes.

If you want coarser oatmeal, stir the oatmeal into the boiling water and cook for just 2 minutes, stirring often. Remove from the heat and cover the pot. Let stand for 2 more minutes.

Serve oatmeal with milk or buttermilk, butter, and maple syrup, molasses, or brown sugar. For a nice contrast, sprinkle uncooked oats over cooked oatmeal.

Steel-Cut Oats

(two servings)

Steel-cut oats are oats that have been through a machine that cuts the whole oat kernels into cream-colored tiny bits. Steel-cut oats (sometimes labeled Scotch or Irish oatmeal) are chewy and capture more of the good oat taste than rolled oats. They take longer to cook, but if you are an oat lover, *please* try these.

2½ cups water
¼ teaspoon salt
1 cup steel-cut oats

Mix the water, salt, and oats together in the top of a double boiler. Cook, covered, over simmering water, stirring occasionally, for 1 hour. Remove from the heat and serve.

A delicious way of cooking steel-cut oat porridge is to combine water, salt, and oats and put overnight in a Crock-Pot or in a covered pot in a 225°F oven. In the morning remove the cover. Do not stir, or the oatmeal will lose some of its delicate, translucent creaminess. Carefully spoon the servings into bowls.

Another way of cooking oats is to shake 1 cup of oats into 3 cups of boiling water without stirring, boil for 5 minutes, and remove from the heat. Let the oats sit all night, covered, in a double boiler or in another larger pan in very hot water. In the morning heat the water in the bottom of the double boiler or larger pot, and let the oatmeal get hot for about 15 minutes. (You won't recognize rolled oats cooked in this way. They become jellylike rather than pasty, and their flavor is more distinctly oaty.)

Steel-cut oats cooked overnight with brown sugar stirred in in the morning, and with yogurt flavored with lemon zest (see page 285) spooned over, make a fine meal.

When serving oatmeal, the Scots insist on providing a bowl of cold rich milk or cream on the side; the porridge eater is supposed to take a spoonful of hot cereal and cool it off in the cold milk before guiding it to his mouth. Serving hot milk over hot cereal is unpardonable in Scotland.

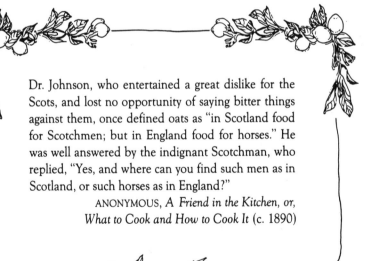

Dr. Johnson, who entertained a great dislike for the Scots, and lost no opportunity of saying bitter things against them, once defined oats as "in Scotland food for Scotchmen; but in England food for horses." He was well answered by the indignant Scotchman, who replied, "Yes, and where can you find such men as in Scotland, or such horses as in England?"

ANONYMOUS, *A Friend in the Kitchen, or, What to Cook and How to Cook It* (c. 1890)

COLD CEREALS

Completely cooked, ready-to-eat cold cereals are the invention of a band of nineteenth-century health food enthusiasts centered in a sanatorium in Battle Creek, Michigan. They shredded, baked, rolled, and puffed various grains, and started the breakfast cereal industry that is still going strong today.

The best cold cereals, and the best healthy buys, are the plain old basics invented long ago: shredded wheat, Grape-Nuts, Cheerios—and any other whole grain cereals with a short list of ingredients on the box and little or no added sugar and salt. I have never been crazy about cold cereals for breakfast, but for people who love air and crunch they are hard to beat. Just buy them plain and basic and sweeten them yourself—it's economical *and* healthy. I like to eat shredded wheat sometimes—I toast it up in the oven for a few minutes and serve it warm with a little butter. Cornflakes are good toasted, too. Cornflakes are also good crumbled up as a coating for French toast (see J.B.'s French Toast, page 40), in puddings and custards, and as a lining for pie shells to prevent the bottom crust from getting soggy.

Granola

(about five cups)

If you think that your own granola will be just the same as what you can buy, you have to try this recipe. The gain in fresh flavor is tremendous and the cost is about a third of store-bought granola.

4 cups mixed flakes	½ cup honey
(oats, rye, barley, wheat, rice)	½ cup (1 stick) butter, melted
Salt to taste	1 cup roughly chopped walnuts
1 teaspoon nutmeg	

Put the flakes in a large bowl and sprinkle with a little salt and the nutmeg. In a small bowl, stir the honey into the butter and blend well. Pour the honey syrup over the flakes and toss until they are well coated.

Spread the mixture on foil in a single layer on a baking sheet. Bake in a preheated 300°F oven for about 20 to 30 minutes, or until the flakes begin to look golden, turning the cereal every 10 minutes with a spoon or a spatula. Be careful not to overbake. The flakes will seem a little sticky when done, but they will crisp as they cool. Stir in the walnuts after baking. Store the granola in plastic bags or an airtight container. Use within a month or store in the freezer.

Unsweetened Granola

(about five cups)

Unsweetened granola has its place. I find that it is more versatile than the sweetened kind. I use it all the time in yeast breads and muffins, and over fruit.

4 cups flakes (oats, rye, barley, wheat, and rice — either all of one kind or mixed)	½ cup safflower oil
1¼ teaspoons salt	Optional: 1 teaspoon nutmeg; 2 teaspoons grated orange zest
	1 cup walnuts

Preheat the oven to 300°F.

Combine the flakes, salt, oil, nutmeg, and orange zest in a large bowl. Toss so that the ingredients are well mixed.

Spread the coated flakes on a baking sheet. Bake about 20 to 30 minutes, turning and stirring the flakes around every 10 minutes. Don't overbake — the cereal is done when it is golden all over. The flakes will seem slightly sticky when first removed from the oven, but they become crisp as they cool. Add the walnuts. Store tightly covered or in plastic bags.

Four-Grain Toasted Cereal with Bananas and Pecans

(about five cups)

This granola recipe is a specialty of Bridge Creek Restaurant, the popular Berkeley, California, breakfast establishment.

1 cup each of the following flakes:	½ cup safflower oil
oats, rye, barley, wheat	Salt to taste
⅓ cup sugar	1 cup broken pecans
1 teaspoon nutmeg	Sliced banana to taste

Preheat the oven to 300°F.

Toss the flakes together in a large bowl until they are mixed.

Stir together the sugar, nutmeg, oil, and salt in a small saucepan. Place over medium heat and stir until the sugar dissolves. Pour the sugar mixture over the flakes and toss until each flake is coated.

Spread the flakes in an even layer on a large baking sheet. Bake for about 20 to 30 minutes, turning the flakes every 10 minutes with a spoon or spatula. Be careful not to overbake; the cereal is done when it is slightly golden. The flakes may seem slightly sticky when they are first removed from the oven, but they become crisp as they cool. Mix in the pecans and serve with sliced banana. Store in an airtight container.

Original Bircher Muesli

(one serving)

Muesli is a Swiss word that means mush. Back in 1895, a Dr. Bircher-Benner invented this combination of fruit and cereal and demonstrated its nutritional value when he successfully treated children with rickets by feeding them Bircher muesli three times a day. It is delicious with fresh strawberries, raspberries, or loganberries in season; and any time of year you can add raisins and chopped hazelnuts and almonds.

1 heaping tablespoon rolled oats
3 tablespoons water
1 tablespoon cream
1 tablespoon honey

1 tablespoon lemon juice
1 small apple
1 tablespoon blackberries

Soak the oats and water in a small bowl overnight.

Just before serving, stir the cream, honey, and lemon juice into the oat mixture. Grate the unpeeled apple and quickly mix into the oats. Add the blackberries. Serve with brown sugar and cream.

Muesli Ballymaloe

(about eight cups)

This is a good recipe from the Allens at Ballymaloe Cooking School in County Cork, Ireland.

8 large shredded wheat biscuits,
   crumbled
2 cups rolled oats
½ cup bran
¾ cup wheat germ

½ cup raisins
⅓ cup nuts
2 tablespoons lecithin
   (available in health food stores)
½ cup brown sugar

Put all the ingredients in a large bowl, toss, and mix. Store in an airtight jar.

Serve in the Swiss way, by soaking the muesli first in yogurt, milk, or cream, grating apples into it, and adding lots of berries or other fruit; or serve as you would any cold cereal, with milk.

Doughnuts and Fritters

Raised Doughnuts
   Jelly Doughnuts or Berlins
Doughnut Glaze
Baked Doughnuts
Buttermilk Breakfast Doughnuts
Dewey Buns
Fruit Fritters
Calas

Homemade doughnuts and fritters have their very own marvelous character, totally unlike anything you can buy out and about. If you've never known the glory of fresh homemade doughnuts and fritters, with their outside crispness and inside buttery rich crumb, get a deep-fat thermometer (the only special piece of equipment you need) and give it a try. Frying at home is a bit of a luxury because you really have to use fresh fat or oil every time: no matter how you try to clarify it, used fat tastes tired. But you shouldn't miss out on giving friends and family (and, most especially, yourself) the opportunity to taste hot, freshly fried doughnuts.

For those with an incurable fear of frying, this chapter has a recipe for wonderful oven-baked doughnuts; but frying is much simpler than you might think. You can fry doughnuts in quite a small amount of fat—a depth of an inch to an inch and a half is plenty in a skillet. You'll have to make one or two test doughnuts before you really get the hang of it—just to know whether you're cooking them too fast or too slowly.

Raised Doughnuts

(about thirty doughnuts)

This is a dough you'll be glad to meet. It is soft and easy to handle, and it turns out light, airy doughnuts.

1/3 cup milk, warmed	2 eggs
1 package dry yeast	4 cups all-purpose flour,
1 cup water	approximately
1/4 cup vegetable shortening	1 1/2 teaspoons salt
1/2 cup sugar plus about 1 cup	1 1/4 teaspoons mace
sugar for sprinkling	Vegetable oil for frying

Put the warm milk in a mixing bowl and add the yeast; stir and let dissolve for about 5 minutes.

Put the water in a small saucepan and bring to a boil. Add the shortening and 1/2 cup sugar, stir until they have dissolved, and remove from the heat. When the water mixture has cooled to warm, add to the yeast mixture. Stir in the eggs and 2 cups flour. Beat well. Add 2 more cups flour and the salt and mace. Stir until well mixed. Add only enough more flour to make a manageable dough; it should be very soft. Turn onto a lightly floured board and knead until smooth and elastic. Place in a large greased bowl, cover, and let rise until double in bulk.

Punch down and put the dough on a lightly floured surface. Roll it out 1/2 inch thick, and then cut out the doughnuts using a 2-inch cutter. Place the doughnuts on a piece of waxed paper or greased baking sheet about 1 inch apart. Let rise until light, about 1 hour.

Heat the oil to between 365°F and 375°F. Fry only about 3 doughnuts at a time—don't crowd the pan. Fry until golden on each side. Remove and pat free of excess oil on paper towels. Roll in the remaining 1 cup of sugar. Or let cool and coat with a sugar glaze.

Jelly Doughnuts or Berlins   Roll out the dough ¼ inch thick. Cut out 2- or 2½-inch rounds. On half of the rounds put about ½ teaspoon jelly. Beat 1 egg white just until it is slightly foamy. Brush the beaten egg white around the edges of all the rounds, cover each round with jelly on it with a plain round, and seal together, pinching the edges. Proceed to fry as directed on page 98. Dust with confectioners' sugar after patting dry of any excess oil.

Doughnut Glaze

(covers a dozen doughnuts)

Mix 2 cups confectioners' sugar with ⅓ cup hot water. Stir until smooth. Put the glaze in a shallow bowl. While the doughnuts are freshly made and hot, dunk all sides of each doughnut in the glaze. If the glaze thickens, thin out with a teaspoon or so of hot water.

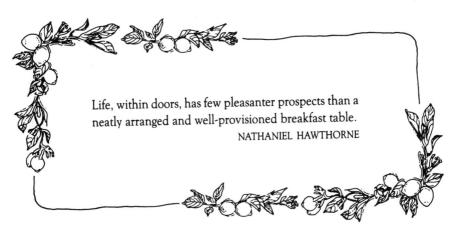

Life, within doors, has few pleasanter prospects than a
neatly arranged and well-provisioned breakfast table.
NATHANIEL HAWTHORNE

Baked Doughnuts

(about two dozen doughnuts plus holes)

If you wish to avoid the deep-frying method, baked doughnuts are the ticket. Light and tender, brushed with butter and rolled in cinnamon sugar, from start to finish these take a little under two hours to make. They freeze well.

2 packages dry yeast
1/3 cup warm water (105°F)
1 1/2 cups milk
1/3 cup vegetable shortening
1/4 cup sugar
2 teaspoons salt
2 teaspoons nutmeg
   (freshly grated if possible)

2 eggs, lightly beaten
4 1/2 cups all-purpose flour,
   approximately
1/2 cup (1 stick) butter, melted
1 cup sugar mixed with
   1 teaspoon cinnamon

Sprinkle the yeast over the warm water in a small bowl and let dissolve for 5 minutes.

Put the milk and shortening in a saucepan and heat until the shortening is melted. Cool to lukewarm.

Put the yeast in a large mixing bowl and add the milk mixture, stir in the 1/4 cup sugar, the salt, nutmeg, eggs, and 2 cups flour. Beat briskly until well blended. Add the remaining flour and beat until smooth. Cover the bowl and let double in bulk, about 1 hour.

Dust a board generously with flour and turn the dough onto it. This dough is soft and needs enough flour on the board to prevent sticking, but it is easy to handle. Pat the dough into a circle about 1/2 inch thick. Use a 3-inch doughnut cutter and cut out the doughnuts, placing them (and the doughnut holes) on greased baking sheets, 1 inch apart. These don't spread much; they rise. Preheat the oven to 450°F. Let the doughnuts rest and rise for 20 minutes, uncovered.

Bake about 10 minutes, or a little longer, until they have a touch of golden brown. Remove from the oven. Have ready the melted butter and a brush. On a sheet of waxed paper spread the cinnamon sugar. Brush each doughnut and doughnut hole with butter and roll in the cinnamon sugar. Serve hot.

Buttermilk Breakfast Doughnuts
(about two dozen doughnuts)

These doughnuts are lightly spiced, round and fat, crisp on the outside and tender on the inside.

1/4 cup vegetable shortening	1 teaspoon baking soda
1 cup sugar plus sugar for sprinkling	1/2 teaspoon cinnamon
2 eggs	1/2 teaspoon mace
3/4 cup buttermilk	1/2 teaspoon nutmeg
3 1/2 cups all-purpose flour	1 1/2 teaspoons salt
2 teaspoons baking powder	Oil for frying

Put the shortening and 1 cup sugar in a large mixing bowl and beat to blend. Add the eggs and beat well. Add the buttermilk and blend.

Put the flour, baking powder, baking soda, cinnamon, mace, nutmeg, and salt in a mixing bowl and stir with a fork until all the ingredients are well mixed. Add the flour mixture all at once to the shortening mixture and beat just until mixed.

Lightly flour a board and turn out the dough. Roll out the dough 1/2 inch thick. Cut the doughnuts out with a 2 1/2- to 3-inch doughnut cutter and place on a sheet of waxed paper. Reroll the scraps and cut out more doughnuts until you run out of dough.

Heat the oil to between 365°F and 375°F. Drop 3 or 4 doughnuts into the hot oil—don't crowd the pan. Fry each side about 2 minutes and turn over with a slotted spoon or wire skimmer. Remove and place on paper towels. Pat to remove any excess oil, and sprinkle sugar over the doughnuts.

Dewey Buns

(eighteen buns)

Dewey Buns are plump squares of light dough filled with vanilla cream. A Dewey Bun business could make someone rich.

1 cup milk, warmed
1/3 cup granulated sugar
1 teaspoon salt
1/4 cup vegetable oil
3 cups all-purpose flour
1 package dry yeast
3/4 teaspoon nutmeg
1 egg
Oil for frying

Dewey Cream
1 egg white
2 1/2 cups confectioners' sugar
4 tablespoons (1/2 stick) butter,
   room temperature
1 tablespoon nonfat dry milk
   (this stabilizes the cream)
1 tablespoon vanilla extract
1/4 teaspoon salt
1/2 cup heavy cream

Confectioners' sugar for dusting

Mix the warm milk with the sugar, salt, and oil and stir to blend.

Stir together 2 cups flour, dry yeast, and nutmeg in a mixing bowl. Add the milk mixture and beat for about 3 minutes. Add the egg and remaining 1 cup flour and beat for 2 minutes. Cover and refrigerate for 4 to 8 hours, or overnight.

Lightly dust a board with flour and turn the dough onto it. Roll the dough into a rectangle about 1/4 inch thick. Cut the dough into squares that are 2 1/2 by 3 inches. Heat oil to about 365°F. Fry the squares, a few at a time, until golden on both sides (it takes about 1 minute on each side). Put the buns on paper towels and pat free of excess oil.

Make the Dewey Cream by putting the egg white, confectioners' sugar, and butter in a mixing bowl. With an electric mixer, beat 3 minutes on high speed, until smooth. Stir the nonfat dry milk, vanilla, and salt into the cream and add to the sugar mixture. Beat until smooth and creamy.

To assemble and fill the buns, cut them in half lengthwise and, using a spoon, scoop out a small shallow pocket from the inside of one of the halves. The pocket should be large enough to hold 1½ table-spoons filling. Fill with Dewey Cream and thinly spread the cream out to the edges. Put the two halves together and gently press the bun edges so that the halves will bind. Sift confectioners' sugar over each side of the bun.

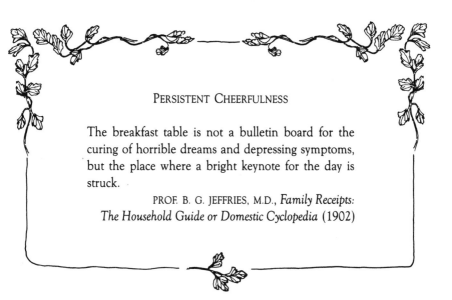

PERSISTENT CHEERFULNESS

The breakfast table is not a bulletin board for the curing of horrible dreams and depressing symptoms, but the place where a bright keynote for the day is struck.

PROF. B. G. JEFFRIES, M.D., *Family Receipts: The Household Guide or Domestic Cyclopedia* (1902)

Fruit Fritters

(six servings)

Fruit Fritters are special. One doesn't make them often and they are not easily found in shops or restaurants, except in New Orleans, where they are called beignets. Fruit Fritters are pieces of fresh fruit dipped in fritter batter, fried to a golden crispness, and sprinkled with confectioners' sugar. Eaten hot, they are wonderful. Most fresh fruits make good fritters. Fruit Fritters are sometimes served with a little maple syrup.

1 egg, separated
3 tablespoons vegetable oil
¾ cup flat beer
1 cup all-purpose flour
½ teaspoon salt
Any combination of the follow-
    ing fruits: apples, ripe and firm,
    peeled, cored, cut into ¼-inch
    slices; bananas, ripe and firm,
peeled, cut into ½-inch slices;
apricots or peaches, ripe and
rather firm, peeled and pitted,
cut into ½-inch slices;
pineapple, rind removed,
cut into ½-inch slices,
    2 inches long
Lemon juice or sugar
Vegetable oil for frying

Put the egg yolk, oil, and beer in a blender, food processor, or bowl and blend thoroughly. Add the flour and salt and beat until smooth. Cover the container with plastic wrap and let rest for at least 1 hour.

Prepare the fruit and taste. If the fruit lacks tartness or sweetness, sprinkle with lemon juice or sugar.

Beat the egg white until stiff but moist. Fold the white into the fritter batter.

Heat approximately 1½ cups vegetable oil in a 10-inch skillet to 370°F. Gently pat each piece of fruit dry of lemon juice or any liquid. Dip each piece of fruit in the batter to coat completely, and put it into the hot oil. If the batter becomes dark brown within a few seconds, remove the skillet from the heat and turn the heat down a little. Cook about 20 seconds, turn the fritter over with a slotted spoon, and cook another 20 seconds, until golden.

Pat the fritters dry of oil on paper toweling, and sprinkle with confectioners' sugar. Keep the fritters warm in a 250°F oven until you have fried enough to serve. You may have to fry a few fritters before they are satisfactory — that is, until you get the hang of it.

Calas

(approximately thirty-two 3-inch fritters)

Calas are a classic rice fritter from New Orleans. Generations ago in the French Quarter, the black Creole cala women would walk through the streets in the morning with large covered bowls on their heads filled with the hot fritters, calling out, "Belles calas!"

1½ cups water	Optional: 1 teaspoon grated
½ cup long grain white rice	lemon zest
1 teaspoon salt, approximately	1 teaspoon nutmeg
½ cup warm water (105°F)	1½ cups all-purpose flour
2 packages dry yeast	Vegetable oil for frying
3 eggs	Confectioners' sugar for sprinkling
⅓ cup sugar	

Bring the 1½ cups water to a boil. Stir in the rice and salt, lower the heat, cover the pot, and cook for about 25 minutes, longer than you usually cook rice, so the rice will be mushy. If there is any liquid left in the rice, drain well. Mash the rice with a fork.

Put the ½ cup warm water in a bowl, sprinkle the yeast over, stir, and let dissolve for 5 minutes. Add the yeast to the lukewarm rice, stir well, cover with plastic wrap, and let stand overnight.

Put the eggs in a bowl and beat well. Beat in the sugar, optional lemon zest, nutmeg, and 1 cup flour. Add the mixture to the rice mixture and beat well for 2 minutes. Add the remaining ½ cup flour and beat well. Taste and add more salt if needed. Cover the bowl and let rise for 30 minutes.

Into a large sauté pan pour vegetable oil to about 1½ inches deep and heat to about 370°F. Drop the batter by heaping tablespoons into the hot oil. I find that you have to make 2 or 3 calas in order to adjust the temperature of the oil. At too high a temperature, they will overfry and get too brown on the outside while remaining raw in the center. Too low, and they will absorb too much oil without coloring. Fry a few at a time, without crowding the pan, for about 1 minute on each side, then turn over with a slotted spoon and fry until golden. Remove the calas to paper towels and pat free of excess oil. Sprinkle with confectioners' sugar and keep warm in a 200°F oven. Serve warm.

Griddling

Plain Pancakes
   Fresh Berry
   Fresh Fruit
   Dried Fruit
   Granola or Nut
Buttermilk Pancakes
   Rye Buttermilk
   Whole Wheat Buttermilk
   Yellow Cornmeal Buttermilk
Bridge Creek Heavenly Hots
Don Chappellet's Zeppelin Pancakes
Lemon Pancakes
Ginger Pancakes
Bridge Creek Spiced Quince Pancakes
Banana Oat Cakes
Bridge Creek Oatmeal Pancakes
Thin Yellow Cornmeal Pancakes
Cornmeal Rye Pancakes
Wheat Crumb Pancakes
Buckwheat Pancakes
Brown Rice Pancakes
Baked German Pancake (or Dutch Babies)
Apple Pancake
Sour Milk Pancakes or Waffles
Raised Waffles
Classic Waffles
   Waffles with Fresh Fruit and Berries
   Strawberry Whipped Cream Waffles
   Waffles with Chopped Nuts
   Cornmeal, Buckwheat, or Rye Flour Waffles
Whole Wheat Buttermilk Waffles
Whole Wheat Granola Waffles

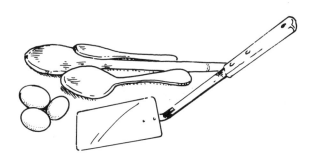

All of the recipes in the griddling family have similar batters, and they are cooked quickly on a very hot surface with very little fat. Time was, every kitchen had a griddle; nowadays most people don't have that extra piece of equipment. But a skillet or frying pan works fine, and a nonstick pan, like an old-fashioned soapstone griddle, requires no fat.

I wonder why pancakes and waffles aren't served at home more often. They certainly are never as good anywhere else, and they are quick and easy to make. Many of these recipes can be prepared the night before or can be assembled very quickly in the morning. Griddlecakes or waffles make a good, sustaining hot breakfast that hits the spot on a cold winter morning, and in the summertime they are great with fresh fruits and berries.

Waffle and pancake batters usually keep well for a couple of days in the refrigerator, but be sure to taste them before use. At refrigerator temperature, batters will thicken somewhat; to thin them out, add a tablespoon or more of milk. They should never be so thick that they aren't pourable and spreadable.

Plain Pancakes

(two dozen 4-inch pancakes)

This basic pancake tastes better than all the others I've tried. Like any good recipe, it is versatile: you can add fresh berries, fruit, granola, spices, and flavors. Pancake batter and waffle batter differ only in that waffle batter is usually thinner. Add a little more liquid to pancake batter and it will cook up as a good, self-respecting waffle.

2 eggs	1 tablespoon sugar
5 tablespoons butter	4 teaspoons baking powder
1 cup milk	¾ teaspoon salt
1¼ cups all-purpose flour	

Beat the eggs in a mixing bowl until they are thoroughly blended. Put the butter and the milk in a small saucepan and warm over low heat until the butter has melted. Set aside and allow to cool a little — you don't want to add this mixture to the eggs while it is very hot or it will cook the eggs. Stir the butter mixture into the eggs and mix well. Put the flour, sugar, baking powder, and salt into a bowl and stir with a fork until well mixed.

Pour the egg mixture into the flour mixture and stir only until the dry ingredients are well moistened. Don't overmix.

Heat a griddle or skillet until a few drops of water dance on it, then lightly film with grease. Drop 2 or 3 tablespoons of batter for each pancake onto the griddle (a 12-inch griddle will hold 4 pancakes) and cook until bubbles break on the surface. Turn the pancake over and cook another 30 seconds, or until the bottom is lightly browned. Serve the pancakes hot.

Fresh Berry Pancakes   Using 2 cups berries (raspberries, strawberries, blueberries, etc.), make sure they are trimmed, cleaned, cut into the desired size, and ready in a bowl by the griddle. Sprinkle 2 to 3 tablespoons of berries on the top of each pancake after the pancake has cooked to the point where the bubbles are breaking on the top, gently pressing the berries down a trifle with a spatula. Turn the pancake over and finish cooking for about 30 seconds, or until set.

Fresh Fruit Pancakes   Use 2 cups of peeled and trimmed fresh fruit (banana, peach, apricot, or orange), cut into small pieces. Follow the directions for Fresh Berry Pancakes.

Dried Fruit Pancakes   Use 2 cups of dried fruit (prunes, dates, raisins, pears, apricots, peaches). Put the dried fruit in a bowl and pour boiling water over. Allow to stand for 10 minutes, drain well, and then chop into small pieces. Follow the cooking directions for Fresh Berry Pancakes.

Granola Pancakes or Nut Pancakes   Add 1 cup granola (see page 90 for homemade granola) or 1 cup chopped walnuts or pecans to the pancake batter and cook as directed in the basic recipe.

Buttermilk Pancakes

(fourteen 3-inch pancakes)

Among buttermilk pancakes, I don't think you can beat these. They are slightly sourish and light, easy to make, and the batter holds well for several days in the refrigerator.

1 cup buttermilk
1 egg, room temperature
3 tablespoons butter, melted

¾ cup all-purpose flour
½ teaspoon salt
1 teaspoon baking soda

Put the buttermilk, egg, and melted butter in a mixing bowl. Stir briskly until the mixture is smooth and blended.

Stir the flour, salt, and baking soda together in a small bowl so they are well blended. Stir into the buttermilk mixture only until the dry ingredients are moistened—leave the lumps.

Heat a skillet or griddle to medium hot. Grease lightly and spoon out about 3 tablespoons of batter per pancake. Spread the batter with the back of the spoon so it is thinned out a little. Cook until a few bubbles break on top. Turn the pancake over and cook briefly. Keep pancakes warm until enough are cooked to serve.

Rye Buttermilk Pancakes   Use ½ cup all-purpose flour and ¼ cup rye flour.

Whole Wheat Buttermilk Pancakes   Replace up to ½ cup all-purpose flour with an equivalent amount of whole wheat flour.

Yellow Cornmeal Buttermilk Pancakes   Substitute ¼ cup yellow cornmeal for ¼ cup of the flour in the recipe.

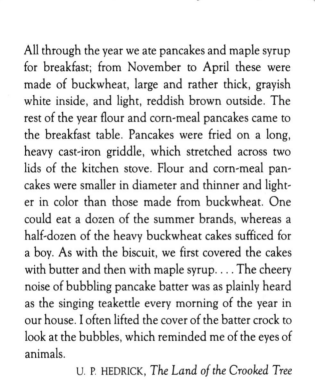

All through the year we ate pancakes and maple syrup for breakfast; from November to April these were made of buckwheat, large and rather thick, grayish white inside, and light, reddish brown outside. The rest of the year flour and corn-meal pancakes came to the breakfast table. Pancakes were fried on a long, heavy cast-iron griddle, which stretched across two lids of the kitchen stove. Flour and corn-meal pancakes were smaller in diameter and thinner and lighter in color than those made from buckwheat. One could eat a dozen of the summer brands, whereas a half-dozen of the heavy buckwheat cakes sufficed for a boy. As with the biscuit, we first covered the cakes with butter and then with maple syrup. . . . The cheery noise of bubbling pancake batter was as plainly heard as the singing teakettle every morning of the year in our house. I often lifted the cover of the batter crock to look at the bubbles, which reminded me of the eyes of animals.

U. P. HEDRICK, *The Land of the Crooked Tree*

Bridge Creek Heavenly Hots

(fifty to sixty dollar-size pancakes)

These are the lightest sour cream silver-dollar-size hotcakes I've ever had—they seem to hover over the plate. They are heavenly and certainly should be served hot.

4 eggs	¼ cup cake flour
½ teaspoon salt	2 cups sour cream
½ teaspoon baking soda	3 tablespoons sugar

Put the eggs in a mixing bowl and stir until well blended. Add the salt, baking soda, flour, sour cream, and sugar, and mix well. All of this can be done in a blender, if you prefer.

Heat a griddle or frying pan until it is good and hot, film with grease, and drop small spoonfuls of batter onto the griddle—just enough to spread to an approximately 2½-inch round. When a few bubbles appear on top of the pancakes, turn them over and cook briefly.

Don Chappellet's Zeppelin Pancakes

(about eighteen 6-inch pancakes)

Don Chappellet, owner of Pritchard Hill Vineyards, perfected this recipe while raising six children for whom he regularly made pancakes on Sunday mornings. I call them zeppelin pancakes because they are very light.

2 eggs, separated
1½ cups buttermilk
½ cup sour cream
¼ cup (½ stick) butter, melted

1 cup all-purpose flour
¾ teaspoon baking soda
½ teaspoon salt

Mix together the egg yolks, buttermilk, and sour cream in a large bowl until well blended. Add the butter and stir until just mixed. Add the flour, baking soda, and salt. Beat until smooth. Beat the egg whites until stiff but still moist. Gently stir the whites into the batter.

When your griddle or frying pan is moderately hot, film with grease and spoon on about ⅓ cup of batter per pancake (these can be made larger or smaller). Turn them over when little bubbles appear on top and cook briefly on the other side.

This batter keeps well in the refrigerator for several days; it will, however, lose a little of its airiness, so just stir in another beaten egg white before using.

Lemon Pancakes

(twelve 3-inch pancakes)

These pancakes make you sit up and take notice. Serve them with fresh raspberries or raspberry syrup and you will have a summer morning special.

3 eggs, separated
¼ cup all-purpose flour
¾ cup cottage cheese
¼ cup (½ stick) butter, melted

2 tablespoons sugar
¼ teaspoon salt
1 tablespoon grated lemon zest

Separate the eggs and beat the egg whites until they hold stiff peaks. In another bowl, stir together the egg yolks, flour, cottage cheese, butter, sugar, salt, and lemon zest until well mixed. (I use the rotary egg beater I used for beating the egg whites.)

With a large spoon or a spatula, fold the egg whites into the yolk mixture. Gently stir until there are no yellow or white streaks.

Heat a skillet or griddle over medium heat. Grease lightly and spoon out about 3 large tablespoons of batter for each pancake. Cook slowly for about 1½ minutes, then turn the pancake over and cook about 30 seconds. Keep the pancakes warm in a 250°F oven until ready to serve.

Ginger Pancakes

(about two dozen 3-inch pancakes)

There is no mistaking the ginger flavor in these unusual pancakes. Everyone will remember them and ask for them again. Ginger pancakes are at their best served with Green Mango Fool (see page 177).

1½ cups all-purpose flour
1 tablespoon ground ginger
½ teaspoon salt
1 teaspoon baking soda

3 tablespoons butter, melted
1¼ cups buttermilk
1 egg, lightly beaten

Combine the flour, ginger, salt, and baking soda in a mixing bowl. Stir with a fork until the dry ingredients are well mixed. Add the melted butter, buttermilk, and egg all at once and stir only until the batter is completely moistened but still lumpy.

Heat a greased griddle or skillet over medium heat. Using a serving spoon, drop approximately 1½ tablespoons batter onto the griddle — this batter is thick, so spread it a little with the back of the spoon after you have dropped each portion onto the griddle. Cook over medium heat, and turn the pancakes as soon as they hold together when you slide a spatula under them.

Keep the pancakes warm in a low oven until you have made enough to serve, or use the time-honored system of cooking pancakes for all present and doing yours last — in other words, serve as you go.

Bridge Creek Spiced Quince Pancakes

(about two dozen pancakes)

Raw quinces have a rather harsh and almost puckery taste. Stewing them in water and sugar removes that characteristic and brings out their spicy flavor. Enjoy these delectable pancakes for that short time in the autumn when quinces are available—everyone will wonder what the elusive flavor is.

Stewed quince purée
2 large quinces
½ cup water
¼ cup sugar

Batter
1 cup milk
2 tablespoons butter, melted
1 egg
1 cup all-purpose flour
2 teaspoons baking powder
¼ teaspoon ground ginger
¼ teaspoon cinnamon
¼ teaspoon salt

To prepare the quince purée, peel the quinces, remove the cores, then chop the quinces into rough pieces. Place in a saucepan with the water and sugar, cover, and simmer gently for 30 to 40 minutes, until the quinces are tender and the liquid has almost entirely evaporated. Purée in a food processor, or beat with an electric mixer (the mixture should not be perfectly smooth). Allow to cool.

Put the rough purée in a mixing bowl and beat in the milk, butter, and egg. In another bowl, toss together the flour, baking powder, ginger, cinnamon, and salt. Add to the quince mixture and beat until the batter is blended.

Heat a lightly greased skillet over moderate heat. Pour on about 2 tablespoons batter for each pancake, allowing room for them to spread.

Cook until bubbles form on the top and the edges begin to look dry, about 1 minute. If necessary, keep the pancakes warm in a 225°F oven until you have made enough to begin serving.

Banana Oat Cakes

(one dozen pancakes)

I serve these oat cakes with sage sausages, adding a few dates and shelled walnuts to the plate.

About 3 bananas
   (to make 1½ cups, mashed)
¼ teaspoon salt
1½ tablespoons sugar

2 teaspoons lemon juice
1 cup oat flour
   (available in health food stores)
2 tablespoons butter

Put the mashed banana, salt, sugar, and lemon juice in a bowl. Beat until smooth. Stir in the oat flour and blend until smooth.

Heat about 2 tablespoons of butter over low heat in a skillet. From a large spoon, drop about 2 or 3 tablespoons of batter onto the skillet for each pancake. Cook briefly, or until lightly golden on both sides. Serve hot.

Bridge Creek Oatmeal Pancakes

(about twelve 4-inch pancakes)

The buttermilk-soaked oatmeal in these pancakes gives them a nubby texture and an agreeable edge of sourness to their taste. Sometime try using steel-cut oats—they accentuate these qualities. Drizzle a little maple syrup over the top or serve with a helping of warm homemade Applesauce (see page 168) on the side.

2 cups buttermilk	1/3 cup whole wheat flour
2/3 cup oatmeal	1 teaspoon baking soda
1 egg	1/2 teaspoon salt
2 tablespoons brown sugar	2 tablespoons vegetable oil
1/3 cup all-purpose flour	

At least 6 hours before making the pancakes, mix the buttermilk and oats together in a bowl. Cover and refrigerate (overnight is fine).

Put the egg in a mixing bowl and beat well, then stir in the brown sugar and blend. Add the flours, baking soda, salt, oil, and the oatmeal-buttermilk mixture. Stir until thoroughly mixed.

Heat a griddle or skillet until it is good and hot, then film with grease. Drop the batter by tablespoons (about 2 1/2 per pancake) onto the griddle and cook until lightly browned on each side.

Thin Yellow Cornmeal Pancakes

(two dozen 3-inch pancakes)

These light and tasty pancakes become stellar when served with Salsa Verde (see page 284) spooned on top. If you are serving the cornmeal pancakes with Salsa Verde, eliminate the sugar in the recipe.

½ cup yellow cornmeal
½ cup boiling water
½ cup all-purpose flour
½ teaspoon salt
1 tablespoon sugar

1 tablespoon baking powder
1 egg, beaten
¼ cup (½ stick) butter, melted
½ cup milk

Put the cornmeal in a mixing bowl and pour the boiling water over, stirring briskly until well blended. Add the flour, salt, sugar, baking powder, the well-beaten egg, the melted butter, and the milk. Beat the batter until it is thoroughly mixed.

Heat the griddle over medium-high heat (don't cook these pancakes over as high a heat as you would normally use). Film the griddle with grease when it is hot. Use 2 tablespoons batter for each pancake. Cook until bubbles break on top of the pancakes and turn them over. Cook another few minutes, or until the bottoms of the pancakes are lightly browned and set. Serve hot.

Cornmeal Rye Pancakes

(about a dozen 4-inch pancakes)

These pancakes have lots of taste and crunch — rye flour and cornmeal mixed with buttermilk do the trick. Maple syrup was invented for them.

1 cup yellow cornmeal	½ teaspoon baking soda
½ cup rye flour	3 tablespoons butter, melted
1 teaspoon salt	2 cups buttermilk

Mix the cornmeal, rye flour, salt, and baking soda together in a large mixing bowl. Stir in the butter and buttermilk, and mix until blended.

Heat a griddle to medium hot and film with grease. Spoon on about 2 tablespoons batter for each pancake. Cook until a few bubbles form on top, turn the pancakes over, and cook until the bottoms are lightly browned. Serve hot.

Wheat Crumb Pancakes

(about a dozen 5-inch pancakes)

Milk-soaked whole wheat bread crumbs make these pancakes light and wheaty-tasting — such a simple procedure for such a good pancake.

1½ cups fresh whole wheat bread crumbs (from about 2 slices bread)	2 eggs, lightly beaten
1½ cups milk	½ cup all-purpose or whole wheat flour
2 tablespoons butter	½ teaspoon salt
	2 teaspoons baking powder

Put the crumbs in a mixing bowl. Heat the milk and butter until the butter melts and the milk is hot. Pour over the crumbs and let soak for about 5 minutes.

Add the eggs, flour, salt, and baking powder to the crumb mixture and stir until blended.

Heat a griddle or frying pan and then film it with grease. Drop about 2 tablespoons batter on the hot griddle and cook until bubbles appear on the pancakes. Turn them over and allow to brown on the bottom. Keep the pancakes warm in a 225°F oven until enough are cooked to serve.

Buckwheat Pancakes

(about three dozen 3-inch pancakes)

In the wintertime, after the buckwheat crop was in, raised buckwheat pancakes replaced cornmeal and flour pancakes on the breakfast tables of frontier America. Buckwheat has a rustic, nutty flavor that tastes almost primitive to me. Plan ahead when you want to make Buckwheat Pancakes, because they are yeast leavened and take an hour or two to rise (or leave the batter overnight in the refrigerator). Serve with butter and maple syrup, or as they do in Russia (where buckwheat pancakes are called blinis), with caviar and sour cream.

1/2 cup warm water	3/4 cup all-purpose flour
1 package dry yeast	2 eggs
1/2 teaspoon sugar	3 tablespoons butter, melted
1 cup milk, warmed	3 tablespoons sour cream
1 1/2 teaspoons salt	1 tablespoon lemon juice
3/4 cup buckwheat flour	

Put the warm water in a large mixing bowl and sprinkle the yeast and sugar over it. Stir and let stand 5 minutes to dissolve.

Add the milk, salt, and 1/4 cup buckwheat flour and 1/4 cup all-purpose flour. Stir briskly to blend. Cover with plastic wrap and let stand until the batter has doubled in bulk. It will be bubbly and very thin. The rising may take 1 to 2 hours, depending on how warm the room is.

Stir the batter and add the remaining ½ cup buckwheat flour and ½ cup all-purpose flour, eggs, butter, and sour cream. Stir until the batter is smooth. If time allows, let the batter rest again for an hour or so. At this point, you may refrigerate overnight.

Heat a griddle or skillet. Add the lemon juice to the batter and stir to blend. Ladle about 1 tablespoon batter to form a 3-inch pancake. Cook until small bubbles appear on top, turn the pancake over, and cook until the bottom is lightly browned. Serve warm.

Brown Rice Pancakes

(two dozen 3-inch pancakes)

These light, airy pancakes will please anyone who loves rice custards. If you use brown basmati rice, your pancakes will have a distinctive, delicious taste.

2 eggs, separated
½ cup cooked brown rice
½ cup milk
¼ teaspoon salt

3 tablespoons all-purpose flour
1 tablespoon butter, melted
Optional: ½ cup golden raisins

Put the egg yolks in a mixing bowl and beat until light. Stir in the rice, milk, salt, flour, and melted butter. Beat until well mixed.

In another bowl, beat the egg whites until stiff but moist. Gently fold the whites into the yolk mixture. Gently stir in the optional raisins at this point.

Film a hot griddle or the bottom of a hot skillet with a little vegetable oil. Stir the batter and drop about 1 tablespoon of batter per pancake onto the griddle or into the skillet. Cook the pancakes over medium-high heat until golden on the bottom, and turn them over gently (these pancakes *are* slightly delicate, but easy to manage), then cook until the other side is golden. The rice in the batter settles to the bottom of the bowl, so be sure to stir the batter before making more pancakes.

Baked German Pancake (or Dutch Babies)

(one 12-inch Baked German Pancake or four 6-inch Dutch Babies)

This is not a griddled pancake at all, but an eggy batter baked in the oven, like Yorkshire pudding or popovers. A baked German pancake (small ones are called *Dutch* babies for some reason) is dramatic and captivating for children. You wouldn't believe what three eggs can do when beaten with milk and flour — this mixture billows up to unbelievable heights and turns golden. The pancake should be sprinkled with lemon juice and confectioners' sugar and served quickly while hot and high and mighty.

3 eggs, room temperature	2 tablespoons butter, melted
½ cup milk	2 tablespoons lemon juice
½ cup all-purpose flour	Confectioners' sugar
½ teaspoon salt	

Preheat the oven to 450°F. Butter one 12-inch skillet or four 6-inch small skillets (with ovenproof handles) or pans (you can use small pie pans or cake pans).

Break the eggs into a mixing bowl and beat until thoroughly mixed. Add the milk and blend well.

Sift the flour and salt onto a square of waxed paper. Lift the waxed paper up by two corners and let the flour slowly drift into the egg and milk, whisking steadily. Or slowly sift the flour and salt directly into the egg mixture, while whisking to blend and smooth. Add the melted butter and mix briskly so the batter is smooth.

Pour the batter into the pan or pans and bake for 15 minutes at 450°F. If you are baking small pancakes, they will be done after 15 minutes. If you are baking just one big pancake, reduce the heat to 350°F and bake another 10 minutes.

Sprinkle the lemon juice over the pancake (or pancakes) and dust the top(s) with confectioners' sugar. Serve at once.

Apple Pancake

(one puffy 10-inch pancake)

This combination of apples cooked in butter and a great big fluffy baked pancake is more exciting than an apple tart.

6 tablespoons (¾ stick) butter
2 large apples, peeled, cored, and
   sliced (McIntoshes are good)
3 tablespoons lemon juice
¼ teaspoon cinnamon
About 5 tablespoons
   confectioners' sugar (depending
   on the sweetness of the apples)

3 eggs, room temperature
¼ teaspoon salt
½ cup all-purpose flour
½ cup milk

Preheat the oven to 425°F.

Melt the butter in a 10-inch skillet or shallow pan and take off heat. If the handle of the skillet is not ovenproof, wrap it with several layers of foil. Remove 2 tablespoons melted butter and set aside in a small bowl.

Put the apple slices in a large bowl with the lemon juice. Stir the cinnamon into the sugar and sprinkle the sugar mixture over the apple slices. Toss to mix. Put the skillet back on the burner and turn the heat to medium. Add the apples and cook, stirring often, for about 3 or 4 minutes, or until the apples are tender but still hold their shape.

In a separate bowl (or blender, or food processor) combine the eggs, salt, flour, milk, and the reserved 2 tablespoons melted butter. Beat until smooth. Spread the apples evenly over the bottom of the skillet and pour the batter on top. Bake for about 20 minutes, or until golden and puffy. Turn immediately onto a warm platter so the apples are on top. Dust with a little confectioners' sugar and serve at once.

The season of buckwheat cakes has arrived. With buckwheat cakes, country-made sausages, a delicate roll or two, and a cup of Mocha coffee, with cream, one can make a very comfortable breakfast. But the cakes must be light, nicely browned, and hot from the griddle; then eaten with plenty of fresh, golden-hued butter, — and, for those who are not particular about the flavor of their coffee, a spoonful or two of refined syrup may be added; and, for my part, I am sorely tempted, I confess, to use maple-syrup, — and you have a dish good enough for any one. The sausages, too, must be well cooked; if they incline to be a little crispy, reminding one just a trifle of the cracklings of roasted pig, it is not amiss. You should be cautious though, as to where you obtain your sausages; if you have ever so slight an acquaintance with the woman who makes them, it is well, provided you have confidence in her. Confidence in your sausage-maker is an excellent thing. One of the best ways for possessing this confidence is to have your sausages prepared in your own house, with materials furnished by yourself.

BARRY GRAY, *Out of Town, A Rural Episode* (1867)

Sour Milk Pancakes or Waffles

(about two dozen 3-inch pancakes or about ten waffles)

Both pancakes and waffles made with this batter are light and tender. Sour milk adds a slightly sour taste that is quite good with sweet maple syrup. Sour the milk by adding 1 tablespoon white vinegar to every cup of milk, then stir and let stand for 10 minutes.

2 eggs, separated
2 cups sour milk (see above)
2 cups all-purpose flour
1 tablespoon sugar

1 teaspoon salt
1½ teaspoons baking soda
½ cup (1 stick) butter, melted

Put the egg yolks in a mixing bowl and beat well. Stir in the sour milk. In another bowl, put the flour, sugar, salt, and baking soda and stir with a fork until well mixed. Add the flour mixture to the yolk mixture and beat until smooth. Stir in the melted butter and mix until well blended.

Beat the egg whites until stiff but still moist. Gently fold the whites into the batter.

Cook as pancakes on a lightly greased hot griddle or skillet, or as waffles in a hot waffle iron. (This is a thin batter, so you do not have to dilute it to use as a waffle batter.)

WAFFLES

It's so drab to just buy a frozen waffle and put it in the toaster, compared to the satisfaction you can get from lifting your own home-made waffles out of a steaming waffle iron. You can take your time and make yeast-risen waffles or you can make quick waffles with baking powder. Waffles are versatile—they are just as good with sausage as they are with fresh strawberries. A friend remembers the special treat of Sunday supper waffles: his mother would serve a waffle covered with liberally peppered creamed hominy, and a dessert waffle would follow with sliced sugared fruit on top.

One minor problem with cooking waffles is that waffle irons vary in size and shape so it's impossible to give specific instructions about the quantity of batter per waffle or the exact yield of these recipes. However, it generally takes ½ to ¾ cup batter to make one waffle.

Raised Waffles

(about eight waffles)

This recipe, from an early Fannie Farmer cookbook, is still the best waffle I know. The mixing is done the night before and all you have to do in the morning is add a couple of eggs and some baking soda. These waffles are very crisp on the outside and delicate on the inside.

½ cup warm water	1 teaspoon sugar
1 package dry yeast	2 cups all-purpose flour
2 cups milk, warmed	2 eggs
½ cup (1 stick) butter, melted	¼ teaspoon baking soda
1 teaspoon salt	

Use a rather large mixing bowl—the batter will rise to double its original volume. Put the water in the mixing bowl and sprinkle in the yeast. Let stand to dissolve for 5 minutes.

Add the milk, butter, salt, sugar, and flour to the yeast mixture and beat until smooth and blended (I often use a hand-rotary beater to get rid of the lumps). Cover the bowl with plastic wrap and let stand overnight at room temperature.

Just before cooking the waffles, beat in the eggs, add the baking soda, and stir until well mixed. The batter will be very thin. Pour about ½ to ¾ cup batter into a very hot waffle iron. Bake the waffles until they are golden and crisp.

This batter will keep well for several days in the refrigerator.

Classic Waffles

(about eight waffles)

These waffles are crisp, flavorful, and ideal for that spur-of-the-moment breakfast when you haven't had time to make yeast-risen waffles.

2 cups all-purpose flour
1 teaspoon salt
4 teaspoons baking powder
2 tablespoons sugar
2 eggs, room temperature

1½ cups milk, warmed slightly
⅓ cup vegetable shortening, melted
⅓ cup (⅔ stick) butter, melted

Put the flour, salt, baking powder, and sugar in a mixing bowl and stir the mixture with a fork until blended.

In another bowl, beat the eggs well and stir in the milk. Combine with the flour mixture until mixed. Add the melted shortening and butter and beat until blended.

Pour about ½ cup batter into a very hot waffle iron. (It takes from ½ to ¾ cup of batter to make one waffle, depending on the size of your waffle iron.) Bake the waffles until they are golden and crisp. Serve hot.

Waffles with Fresh Fruit and Berries   Berries of all kinds, fresh sliced peaches, nectarines, apricots, and bananas are all delicious with waffles, but they should not be added to the batter or they can alter and spoil the waffle's texture. Fruits and berries are best served on top of hot, cooked waffles, or on the side of the plate.

Strawberry Whipped Cream Waffles These linger in the minds of many as a Sunday morning treat when the family gathered around the breakfast table. They are traditionally served with lightly sweetened whipped cream piled on top of the hot, cooked waffles. With a mound of strawberries on top, this is a glorious sight.

Waffles with Chopped Nuts It is best to add chopped nuts to waffles when they have nearly finished cooking. Sprinkle about 1/4 cup chopped nuts evenly over the top of the waffle about 30 seconds before it is done.

Cornmeal, Buckwheat, or Rye Flour Waffles Substitute 1/2 cup cornmeal, buckwheat flour, or rye flour for 1/2 cup of the all-purpose flour called for in the basic recipe.

Whole Wheat Buttermilk Waffles

(six to eight waffles)

These waffles are appealing because of their tart, wheaty taste. The perfect complement is warm honey—which becomes thin and pours like syrup when heated.

3/4 cup whole wheat flour	2 tablespoons sugar
3/4 cup all-purpose flour	3 eggs
2 teaspoons baking powder	1 1/2 cups buttermilk
3/4 teaspoon baking soda	3/4 cup (1 1/2 sticks) butter, melted
1/2 teaspoon salt	1/4 cup milk, if needed

Put the flours into a mixing bowl and add the baking powder, baking soda, salt, and sugar. Stir with a fork to blend.

In another mixing bowl, beat the eggs until well blended. Stir in the buttermilk and the melted butter (cooled off a little). Add the flour mixture and stir until well mixed—if the batter seems rather thick, add the $1/4$ cup milk to thin it. The batter should flow from the spoon, not plop.

Bake in a hot waffle iron until crisp and golden. Serve hot.

Whole Wheat Granola Waffles

(ten waffles)

Adding granola makes a chewy, tasty, and substantial waffle that soaks up lots of butter and syrup and is delicious served with sliced bananas or melon. Use your own homemade Granola (see page 90) in these waffles and the flavor will be worlds better.

1½ cups granola (without raisins or dried fruit)	1½ cups whole wheat flour
	1 tablespoon baking powder
1¾ cups milk, plus a few tablespoons more if needed	½ teaspoon baking soda
	¼ teaspoon salt
½ cup (1 stick) butter, melted	Melted shortening or oil,
2 eggs	if needed

Stir together the granola and milk in a medium-size mixing bowl and allow to stand for 10 to 15 minutes, until the granola has softened.

Beat the melted butter and eggs into the granola-milk mixture. In a separate bowl, stir together the flour, baking powder, baking soda, and salt. Add to the first mixture and beat just until the batter is blended.

Heat the waffle iron and brush lightly with melted shortening or oil, if necessary. Pour in just enough batter (½ to ¾ cup) to barely fill the grids. Close the iron and cook just until the steaming stops and the waffles are golden. If the batter becomes too thick while standing, stir in a tablespoon or two more milk.

Eggs

Soft-Boiled Egg
Coddled Egg
Hard-Boiled Eggs
Goldenrod Eggs
Scalloped Eggs
Scotch Eggs
Chinese Tea Eggs
Fried Eggs
Knothole Eggs
Poached Eggs
Butter-Crumbed Eggs
Huevos Verdes
Eggs Beatrice
Eggs Benedict
Shirred Eggs
   with Cheese, with Ham or Bacon, with Mixed Herbs
Shirred Lemon Eggs
Buttermilk Baked Egg
Scrambled Eggs
   with Ham; with Bacon;
   and Cheese; and Herbs; and Croutons
Crackered Eggs
Omelets
Filled Omelets
   Ham, Apple, Cheese, Bacon,
   Herb, Mushroom, Jelly, Bread and Butter,
   Smoked Salmon, Caviar, Bridge Creek
Puffy Omelets
   Mushroom, Mexican, Ham or Bacon,
   Cheese, Herb, Jelly or Jam
Frittata with Cheese and Crumbs
Featherbed Eggs
   Apple Ham, Fresh Fruit and Cream Cheese
Oatmeal Soufflé
   Oatmeal Bacon
Lemon Zephyrs

I grew up in the small rural foothill town of La Crescenta, California, in the twenties. I was an only child, and my mother was twenty-seven when I was born (which is like being forty-five today). As a result, she was an anxious mother, always sending away for government pamphlets for advice on how to feed me. One of the things the pamphlets said was that an egg and a glass of goat's milk were perfect whole foods for a growing child. So my father had to get a goat to join the chickens we already kept.

I still love eggs. And if I'm going to have one small thing for breakfast, I cook one egg until it's almost hard, shell it, and have it with lots of pepper on it. I can eat only one hard-boiled egg, but if I'm soft-boiling them I do it by twos, mash them up in a bowl, sprinkle salt over them and a little bit of pepper, and eat them with toast — and that suffices for hours. Where is it written in stone that we always have to be served two eggs cooked the same way? I sometimes serve one butter-crumbed poached egg with one softly scrambled egg. Eggs really do satisfy those nudging little eleven o'clock hunger pangs like no other breakfast food.

Today eggs are more widely available and cheaper than ever before. And the eggs from our big supermarkets have been stored carefully and are fresher than you probably think they are. Once you get your eggs home, you should put them in the refrigerator and keep them there — eggs can deteriorate as much in one day at room temperature as they would in a week in the refrigerator.

It is easy to cook eggs properly if you follow a couple of basic guidelines. With few exceptions, eggs should be cooked slowly, and over low heat, because both egg white and egg yolk coagulate at well below the temperature of boiling water. When cooking an egg in its shell, if you first pierce its large end with an egg-piercing gadget or pushpin, it will help keep the shell from cracking as it cooks. The recipes in this book call for size large eggs, unless otherwise specified.

Soft-Boiled Egg

For a perfect soft-boiled egg, first bring about 4 cups water (enough to cover an egg by at least an inch) to a simmer. Take an egg from the refrigerator, pierce its large end, and lower it with a large spoon into the simmering water. After 3 minutes, half the white will be set and half will be runny and clear. After 4 minutes, two thirds of the white will be set; the rest will be runny. After 5 minutes, the white will be completely set. The yolk will be warm and creamy at each stage. Remove from the water and serve.

Coddled Egg

To coddle an egg, first bring about 4 cups water to a simmer. Take an egg from the refrigerator, pierce its large end, and lower it with a spoon into the simmering water. Remove from the heat, cover the pan, and let it sit for 10 minutes. The white will be delicate and tender.

The breakfast egg was a Victorian institution (only a century old); whatever else there was for breakfast— kidneys, chops, bacon, or kedgeree, with tea or coffee, marmalade or honey— there was always a meek little cluster of boiled eggs, set modestly apart upon a chased silver stand, with their spoons beside them (like St. Ursula's virgins on shipboard).

Really nice homely families kept their little flotilla of breakfast eggs coddled in hot water under a china hen. Many of these hens were beautifully modelled. Our hen is of pure-white china with dull-gold beak, her crimson top-knot is studded with white raised dots, in toadstool pattern, her tail smoothly plumed, and her basket-nest most carefully moulded and touched with gold. She has a pure but friendly eye. There were handsome black hens (like plump matrons in black alpaca). Black hens usually had gold-lustre spots and white wattles. There were naturalistic brown hens on yellow baskets, and rather coarse red-and-white Staffordshire hens on green tub bases.

The bases in all cases held the eggs in hot water, which kept them from going hard and drying up. . . .

Smaller, larger, or less-punctual households had table egg-boilers and "did" their own eggs for themselves as they came down. . . .

"Breakfast trays" and "single gents" had egg-cosies—not today's church-bazaar fancies, but solid thick woollen coats. Cooks today crack the boiled egg on top "to let the steam out," but the old-fashioned idea was to keep the steam in—as a new-laid egg should be steamy and milky within.

According to superstition, empty egg-shells should always be broken up—lest witches make boats thereof.

DOROTHY HARTLEY, *Food in England*

Hard-Boiled Eggs

Take the desired number of eggs from the refrigerator, pierce the large end of each egg with an egg piercer or pushpin, and place them in a saucepan in a single layer. Add enough cold water to completely immerse the eggs to a depth of 1 inch. Bring the water to a boil, reduce the heat, and let simmer for 20 minutes. Remove and place in cold water.

To peel hard-boiled eggs, tap the egg gently all over and crack the shell. Loosen the shell at the larger end and peel it off under running water.

Goldenrod Eggs

(two or three servings)

Goldenrod Eggs are a traditional dish that I learned to make years ago in home economics class (the lesson taught us how to make a cream sauce and how to temper egg yolks). The yolks sieved over the whites are supposed to look like goldenrod. I was very taken with the dish, and once in a blue moon I make it again. It's nutritionally complete, and it's tasty.

4 hard-boiled eggs, shelled	Salt and pepper
2 tablespoons butter	1 raw egg yolk
2 tablespoons flour	2 tablespoons lemon juice
1¼ cups milk (whole or skim)	2 slices buttered toast

Separate the whites and the yolks of the hard-boiled eggs. Dice the whites and set aside. Reserve the yolks.

Put the butter into a small saucepan and melt over medium-low heat. Stir in the flour and cook, stirring constantly, until the butter and flour are well blended; then cook over low heat, stirring, at least 2 minutes more.

Slowly add the milk, stirring constantly, and cook for 5 minutes, stirring until the sauce has thickened. Add salt and pepper to taste. In a small bowl, combine the raw yolk and lemon juice. Stir several tablespoons of the hot sauce into the yolk mixture, then add the yolk mixture to the sauce. Cook another minute or two, until smooth and hot. Add the diced egg whites to the sauce.

Assemble by spooning the sauce over the toast. Using the fine-grating side of a grater or a sieve, rub a yolk or two over each portion. Serve immediately.

Scalloped Eggs

(four servings)

Served with crisp bacon and a baked apple on the side, this makes a good breakfast.

8 tablespoons (1 stick) butter	½ teaspoon freshly grated
3 cups bread crumbs	(or ground) nutmeg
8 hard-boiled eggs, sliced	1½ cups milk
Salt and pepper to taste	

Preheat the oven to 400°F. Butter a round, shallow baking dish; a 9- or 10-inch round glass pie plate would be ideal.

Melt the butter in a large skillet or sauté pan. Add the crumbs and cook over low heat, stirring often until the crumbs are golden and have absorbed the butter.

Spread half of the crumbs evenly over the bottom of the baking dish. Arrange the egg slices over the crumbs. Sprinkle with salt, pepper, and half the nutmeg. Pour the milk evenly over the egg slices and distribute the remaining crumbs evenly over the top. Lightly salt and pepper the top and dust with the rest of the nutmeg. Bake for about 25 minutes. Serve hot.

Scotch Eggs

(eight eggs)

Scotch Eggs are a classic English pub food: hard-boiled eggs encased in sausage, breaded, and deep fried. They are especially wonderful if you use your own sausage meat seasoned with fresh sage and lots of black pepper (see page 197). Buy the smallest eggs you can find—supermarket medium will do. Scotch Eggs are good hot or cold.

3 tablespoons flour	2 eggs, lightly beaten
1 pound sausage meat	8 medium hard-boiled eggs,
1½ cups bread crumbs	shelled
Salt and pepper	Vegetable oil for deep frying

You may do all the preparations the night before and keep the sausage-coated eggs covered in the refrigerator.

Put the flour on a piece of waxed paper or in a shallow dish. Divide the sausage meat into eight pieces. Season the bread crumbs with salt and pepper. Have the beaten eggs and the crumbs in separate shallow dishes.

Roll each hard-boiled egg in flour to coat all over. Flatten each piece of sausage meat in the palm of your hand. Place the egg in the center and press the meat all over the egg. Dip the egg into the beaten eggs and then into the crumbs, rolling the egg to cover all sides.

Use a sauté pan or deep fryer to cook the Scotch Eggs. If you use a sauté pan, fill it with oil 1 inch deep. Heat the oil to 360°F. Slip the coated eggs into the hot oil (don't crowd the pan) and fry until golden on all sides. This will take only a few minutes. Don't let them get dark brown; if the eggs seem to be getting too brown too quickly, take them out and lower the heat, or pull the pan a little off the burner to cool the oil down a bit. Remove and pat dry of oil on paper towels. Serve warm, or refrigerate until needed.

Chinese Tea Eggs

(eight eggs)

These eggs simmer in their shells for an hour and a half so that they become thoroughly infused with the flavors of tea and star anise, and the whites become beautifully marbled. Make Chinese Tea Eggs on those days when you want to try something a little adventurous.

8 hard-boiled eggs
6 cups water
3 tablespoons black tea leaves
   (or 4 tea bags)

2 tablespoons star anise (available in Oriental grocery stores), or
1 tablespoon anise seeds
4 teaspoons salt, approximately

Do not shell the eggs, just lightly tap each one all over to make a network of cracks.

Put the water, tea leaves, star anise, and salt in a saucepan and add the eggs. Bring the liquid to a simmer and cook for 1½ hours. Let the eggs cool in the liquid. They are good warm or cold.

Serve peeled and halved, dome side up, on a bed of hot steamed rice. Surround with wedges of tangerine, lemon, and lime. Squeeze the lemon and lime on the rice and eggs, and pass around a dish with more tangerine wedges.

Fried Eggs

Eggs should be fried with restraint. Fried too fast over high heat, their whites will be tough and rubbery.

Use a heavy, well-seasoned skillet or a nonstick frying pan, large enough so that the eggs aren't crowded. An 8-inch-diameter pan is perfect for two eggs. Heat the pan over medium-low heat. When the pan is hot, add 1 teaspoon butter for each egg and swirl the butter around to coat the bottom. When the butter is melted and starts to foam, carefully crack the eggs into the pan. The white will start to set immediately; make sure it isn't sticking by giving the pan a gentle shake. If necessary, free the egg by sliding a spatula under it. Fried without turning, or *sunny-side-up*, the egg will be done in 3 to 4 minutes; or cover the pan and the egg will be done in 2 to 3 minutes.

For eggs *over easy*, fried on both sides, turn gently with a spatula after 3 to 4 minutes and allow the other side to cook for just a few seconds. For eggs *over hard*, the yolks no longer runny, allow 1 full minute after turning.

For *butter-basted* eggs, use 1 additional tablespoon butter per egg. Proceed as you would for eggs sunny side up, but spoon the extra butter over the top of the eggs as they fry.

Knothole Eggs

(two servings)

A dish to delight a child, but you will smile and relish this, too.

2 slices sandwich bread	2 eggs
2 tablespoons butter	Salt and pepper to taste

Toast the bread lightly. With a circular cutter or a wine glass about 2 inches in diameter, cut a hole out of the center of each slice.

Melt the butter over medium-low heat in a large skillet and put the bread slices side by side in the pan. Crack an egg into each hole, letting the yolk fall into the center. Some of the white will run over the bread and down the side. Turn the heat to low and sprinkle with salt and pepper to taste. Cover the pan and cook gently for 2 or, at the most, 3 minutes, until the whites are barely set. Serve on warm plates.

Poached Eggs

The eggs to be poached will be getting a preliminary short boil. In a saucepan, boil enough water to completely cover the eggs. Gently lower the unshelled eggs into the saucepan. Count to 30 and remove the eggs. This preliminary cooking in the shell will harden the egg white a little so that the egg will hold its shape better as it poaches.

Bring to a simmer 4 cups water and 2 teaspoons cider vinegar in a 10-inch deep-frying pan or sauté pan. If you are poaching more than 4 eggs and need a larger pan, add 1 teaspoon vinegar for each additional 2 cups water. One by one, crack each egg on the edge of the frying pan, open up the shell just over the simmering water, and let the egg fall gently into the water. If the eggs are not totally submerged, spoon the simmering water over them as they poach. They will be ready after 1 to 1½ minutes. Or remove the pan from the heat immediately after adding the eggs, cover, and the eggs will be poached after 4 to 5 minutes.

Remove the eggs with a skimmer or slotted spoon and let them drain on a towel. If you are not using the poached eggs right away, put them directly into a bowl of ice water and refrigerate. They will keep for 2 or 3 days. Reheat them in a bowl of very hot water for about 1 minute.

Butter-Crumbed Eggs

(eight eggs)

In this recipe, poached eggs are dipped first in raw egg, then in crumbs, and fried in butter. It may seem like a lot of trouble, but this recipe is easier than it sounds—and once you taste these eggs, you will agree that they are well worth the effort. There is something divine in this perfect combination of bread, butter, and egg.

8 poached eggs	2 cups fresh bread crumbs
2 raw eggs	Salt and pepper to taste
8 tablespoons (1 stick) butter	

Trim any ragged edges from the poached eggs, and blot them dry.

In a shallow dish, beat the 2 raw eggs with a fork until well blended. Start melting the butter in a large skillet over medium-low heat while you crumb the poached eggs. Salt and pepper the bread crumbs in a shallow bowl.

Have a piece of waxed paper ready so you can place the crumbed eggs on it. I use a small spatula to move the eggs without breaking the tender yolks. Dip each egg into the beaten eggs, then gently coat the top and bottom with the bread crumb mixture. Place the eggs on the waxed paper.

When the butter has melted, slide the eggs one by one into the skillet and fry each side just until lightly golden and watch carefully to see that they don't brown too much. Place on a warm platter and serve.

Huevos Verdes

(four servings)

There is nothing like Salsa Verde, a fresh and lively green sauce, over eggs and tortillas to wake up a sleepy palate.

Salsa Verde (see page 284)
4 flour tortillas, about 8 inches
    in diameter
8 poached eggs, either freshly
    poached or reheated
    (see page 144)

2 cups grated Monterey Jack
    cheese
Fresh cilantro sprigs for garnish

Heat the Salsa Verde, but don't bring to a boil—you want to keep the sauce fresh-tasting. Over high heat on a griddle or in a dry skillet, cook the tortillas until their surfaces blister.

Place a tortilla on each plate and spoon 3 tablespoons of sauce in the center. Place 2 eggs on each sauced tortilla and sprinkle 1/2 cup cheese over each. Place the plates under the broiler for 1 minute (watch closely), until the cheese is just melted. Spoon a tablespoon or two of the sauce on top, add garnish, and serve.

Eggs Beatrice

(four servings)

Eggs Beatrice are a lighter and more delicate version of Eggs Benedict.

8 thin slices ham
8 slices thin-sliced white bread
   (dense, rather than airy bread)

8 poached eggs
1¼ cups Blender Hollandaise

Blender Hollandaise

(1¼ cups)

Hollandaise is more easily made in a blender than a food processor because the container is smaller and the ingredients blend more easily. Be sure to thin this sauce with a little hot water to the point where it flows readily from a spoon. Hollandaise that is too thick will coarsen the dish.

2 egg yolks
2 tablespoons boiling water,
   approximately
1 cup (2 sticks) butter, melted
   and hot

2 tablespoons lemon juice
Salt to taste

Put the yolks in a blender. Blend at low speed for a couple of seconds. Slowly add the boiling water, then very slowly add the hot, melted butter. Be patient at this point—you must pour the butter in the thinnest of streams, almost in fast drops. Add the lemon juice and salt. If the sauce is very thick, add a little more boiling water. Set aside while you are poaching the eggs—don't worry if your sauce is room temperature.

To assemble, put the ham in a small skillet, cover, and place over the lowest possible heat while you make the toast. Put a piece of lightly buttered toast on each warmed plate, cover with 2 slices of ham, then place 2 eggs on the ham. Spoon 3 to 4 tablespoons of hollandaise on top of each serving. Lightly butter and cut the remaining 4 slices of toast and bring to the table. Serve the rest of the hollandaise sauce in a small bowl.

Eggs Benedict   Follow the recipe for Eggs Beatrice but use 8 thin slices of frizzled Canadian bacon instead of ham and substitute 4 English muffins for the bread. Split and toast the muffins and then put them in a low oven while you poach your eggs. Assemble as you would Eggs Beatrice.

Shirred Eggs

Whole eggs gently baked in buttered ramekins are known as shirred eggs. For each egg, melt 1 teaspoon butter in a ramekin in a 325°F oven. Break an egg into each ramekin, salt and pepper it, and bake for 12 minutes, or until the egg is just set. Serve immediately. You may pour 1 teaspoon melted butter or 2 teaspoons cream over the egg before putting it into the oven. Shirred eggs are a convenient dish to serve when you have invited a number of people over for breakfast; you might try cooking a number this way using buttered muffin tins instead of ramekins.

Shirred Eggs with Cheese   Sprinkle 1 tablespoon grated cheese on top of each egg about 3 minutes before the egg has finished baking.

Shirred Eggs with Ham or Bacon   Put 1 tablespoon chopped ham or crisp, crumbled bacon in the bottom of each ramekin before adding the egg.

Shirred Eggs with Mixed Herbs   Put 1 teaspoon finely chopped fresh parsley and ½ teaspoon each dried thyme and marjoram (or any mixture of herbs you like) in the bottom of each ramekin before adding the egg.

Shirred Lemon Eggs

(four eggs)

We think of something citrus as part of morning, and eggs have a special affinity for lemon. The lemon zest enhances the flavor of the eggs and it looks nice, too. Buttered, warm Melba Toast (see page 31) would be good with this dish.

½ cup heavy cream	4 eggs
1½ teaspoons grated lemon zest	Salt and pepper to taste
⅓ cup grated Gouda cheese	1 tablespoon finely minced
(or any mild cheese)	parsley

Preheat the oven to 325°F. Liberally butter four ramekins—they should hold approximately ½ cup each.

Pour 1 tablespoon cream into the bottom of each ramekin. Sprinkle about ¼ teaspoon lemon zest over the cream in each. Divide the cheese evenly among the four ramekins, sprinkling it on top of the cream. Gently drop an egg into each ramekin and add salt and pepper. Measure 1 tablespoon cream and spread it over each egg; scatter a little parsley over the tops. Bake for about 12 minutes, or just until the egg is slightly set. Serve immediately.

Buttermilk Baked Egg

(one egg)

You will be quite taken with what buttermilk does to an egg—it lends a creamy sharpness and yet has fewer calories than an equivalent amount of cream or cream sauce.

1 slice sandwich bread	Salt and pepper to taste
1 egg	¼ cup buttermilk

Preheat the oven to 350°F. Toast the bread lightly. Cut a hole in the center with a 1½-inch circular cutter. Butter an ovenproof dish. Put the toast in it and break open the egg over it so that the yolk falls in the hole in the center. Salt and pepper to taste. Spoon the buttermilk over the egg. Bake for 15 minutes.

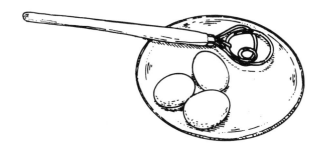

Scrambled Eggs

(two eggs)

2 tablespoons butter	2 eggs
¼ cup water	Salt and pepper to taste

Heat a small frying pan (about 8 inches in diameter) over low heat and add 1 tablespoon butter. In a small saucepan, heat the water with the other tablespoon butter. Break the eggs into a bowl and beat them briskly with a fork for about 10 seconds, until the yolks and whites are mixed. When the butter in the frying pan has melted and has just started to foam, pour in the eggs. Stir them constantly but gently, keeping them moving so that the uncooked liquid egg runs under the curds of coagulating egg. After about 10 seconds, salt and pepper them. After 2 minutes, add 1 to 3 tablespoons hot water and butter and gently stir into the eggs as they finish cooking. Take the eggs off the heat just before they have reached the consistency you prefer; they will continue to cook for a few seconds. Dish up onto warm plates.

Scrambled Eggs with Ham   Add ¼ cup chopped ham to the scrambled eggs as they finish cooking.

Scrambled Eggs with Bacon   Add ¼ cup crisp, crumbled bacon to the eggs just as they finish cooking.

Scrambled Eggs and Cheese   Sprinkle ¼ cup grated cheese onto the eggs as they finish cooking.

THE BREAKFAST BOOK 151

Scrambled Eggs and Herbs To the beaten eggs, add 1 teaspoon chopped fresh parsley and 1 teaspoon of one or more of the following herbs: tarragon, chervil, chives, savory, borage (fresh or dried).

Scrambled Eggs and Croutons Fry ½ cup small bread cubes in 2 tablespoons butter until they are brown and crisp. Add to the eggs as they finish cooking.

Crackered Eggs

(four servings)

It is amazing that these ingredients result in such a moist, savory dish. Serve the wedges with syrup, or spread lightly with preserves, or have them plain with bacon or ham.

2 eggs	3 tablespoons butter
1 cup milk	Pepper to taste
20 saltines	

Whisk the eggs and milk together thoroughly. Crumble the crackers and stir them into the egg mixture. Let this sit for about 10 minutes.

Melt the butter in a 10-inch skillet over medium-low heat. Pour the mixture into the skillet, distributing the bits of cracker evenly over the bottom of the pan with a fork. Cook slowly for about 2 or 3 minutes, or until the bottom of the mixture is lightly browned. Using a large spatula, cut the round in two and turn over first one half and then the other. Allow to cook for another minute or two, until the other side has browned lightly. Sprinkle with pepper and cut into wedges.

Omelets

(*one serving*)

I make omelets in a rather casual way. You don't need a special omelet pan—just about any pan with a nonstick surface will work. (By the way, I find that the cast-iron pans you buy today don't temper well and the egg sticks.) The right size pan for a two- or three-egg omelet is one with a bottom diameter of 8 inches. If you have never made an omelet before, first read this recipe all the way through—the whole process takes only about a minute.

2 eggs
Salt and pepper to taste
2 teaspoons butter

Break the eggs into a small bowl, add salt and pepper, and whisk vigorously with a fork for about 10 seconds, just enough to thoroughly blend yolks and whites. Put an 8-inch nonstick skillet over high heat. When it is quite hot, add the butter and tilt the pan, swirling the butter in all directions to coat the bottom and sides. The butter should not get brown. When the foaming butter starts to subside, pour in the eggs. Let them set about 5 seconds. Using a spatula, pull the cooked egg from the edges of the pan toward the center, allowing the liquid egg to run under onto the hot pan. After about 20 seconds, while the eggs are still very moist and creamy, push the omelet toward one side of the pan, and then with a spatula fold half the omelet over the other half. Let the omelet cook for 5 seconds more to lightly brown the bottom, and then quickly tilt the pan upside down over a plate so the omelet falls out bottom side up. You can pat the omelet into shape with your hands and draw a piece of butter over the top to make it shiny.

Filled Omelets

If you fill your omelet, mind the proportion of filling to egg. The tender, softly cooked egg is spoiled by too much filling. For every 2-egg omelet, 4 tablespoons or ¼ cup filling is just right, with few exceptions. Never add a very wet filling: the liquid dilutes the egg and makes it puddly. Any of the following variations is delicious:

Ham Omelet   Add ¼ cup finely chopped ham to the beaten eggs.

Apple Omelet   Fill with ¼ cup applesauce or cooked diced apples.

Cheese Omelet   Spread ¼ cup grated cheese over the eggs just before folding.

Bacon Omelet   Add ¼ cup crisp, crumbled bacon to the beaten eggs.

Herb Omelet   Mix 2 teaspoons finely chopped parsley with 1 teaspoon fresh sage, tarragon, thyme, or savory and add to the beaten eggs.

Mushroom Omelet   Sauté ½ cup raw sliced or chopped mushrooms in 2 tablespoons butter and add to the eggs just before folding.

Jelly Omelet   Put about ¼ cup of your favorite jelly onto the eggs just before folding over.

Bread and Butter Omelet   Fry ½ cup small bread cubes in 2 tablespoons butter until lightly browned and crisp. Sprinkle the croutons onto the eggs just before folding over.

Smoked Salmon Omelet   Just before you fold over the omelet place 1 thin slice smoked salmon and 2 tablespoons cream cheese or farmer's cheese onto the eggs.

Caviar Omelet   Spoon 2 tablespoons salmon roe or caviar over the eggs before folding.

Bridge Creek Omelet   Put ⅓ cup grated Tillamook cheese and enough thick-sliced bacon that has been cooked crisp and cut into ½-inch pieces to make ⅓ cup onto the eggs before folding them over.

Puffy Omelets

(two servings)

I like these airy, foamy omelets—they look so grand and filling. The trick is not to cook them until they are too dry. Breakfast Baps (see page 19) and a puffy omelet make a good breakfast team.

3 eggs, separated
¼ teaspoon salt, or to taste
¼ teaspoon pepper

2 tablespoons butter
Filling (see following recipes)

Preheat the oven to 400°F. For a three-egg omelet, use a 10-inch skillet with sloping sides—they usually measure about 8 inches across the bottom. You may cook the omelet completely on top of the stove, but I prefer the oven finish because it is easier to keep the omelet moist.

Briskly beat the yolks a few seconds, until they are thoroughly blended. Sprinkle salt over the whites and beat them until they are stiff but moist. Fold the yolks and whites together until they are barely incorporated.

Put the butter into the skillet over high heat. When the butter begins to foam, pour the eggs into the skillet. Shake the pan a little, or gently spread the omelet with a spatula. Sprinkle the pepper over the eggs. Allow the omelet to cook for about 1 minute, or until the bottom is brown. Remove from the stove and put into the oven. Have the filling ready and the plates warm. Take a look at the omelet after a minute or so and press the top with your finger. It is done when it is spongy, but moist. It takes about 3 minutes to set.

Remove from the oven and quickly spread the filling across the center and fold the omelet in half with a spatula. If you aren't using any sauce to cover the omelet, spread a little butter over the top. Serve at once.

Mushroom Omelet

4 tablespoons (½ stick) butter	¼ cup finely chopped parsley
2 cups fresh mushrooms, wiped clean and sliced	Optional: Goldenrod Eggs sauce (see page 138)
Salt and pepper to taste	

Melt the butter in a skillet, add the mushrooms, and stir over low heat just until they begin to soften and change color. Salt and pepper them and set aside; stir the parsley into the mushrooms just before you are ready to use them. Put half the mushrooms in the center of the omelet before folding. If you are using the optional sauce, stir the remaining mushrooms into it and spoon the sauce on top of the omelet just before serving. If no sauce is used, spoon the mushroom-parsley mixture over the top.

Mexican Omelet

1 cup grated Monterey Jack
  cheese

1 cup Salsa Verde (see page 284),
  warmed

Sprinkle the cheese and ½ cup sauce in the center of the omelet before it is folded in half. Spoon the remaining ½ cup sauce over the omelet before serving.

Ham or Bacon Omelet

1 cup finely chopped ham or
  crisp, crumbled bacon

Freshly ground black pepper
  to taste

Just before folding the omelet in half, spread the ham or bacon down the center. Grind lots of black pepper over it. Fold the omelet and grate a little more pepper on top before serving.

Cheese Omelet

1 cup grated Cheddar,
  Monterey Jack, or any favorite
  melting cheese

¼ cup finely chopped parsley

Sprinkle the cheese down the center of the omelet just before folding in half. Sprinkle half the parsley on top of the cheese and the rest on top of the omelet after folding it.

Herb Omelet

1 tablespoon finely chopped fresh
   herbs; or half as much dried
   herbs (try an equal mixture
   of parsley, thyme, and sweet
   marjoram, or your favorite
   herb combination)

½ cup sour cream
2 tablespoons milk

Sprinkle 2 teaspoons of herbs down the center of the omelet and spoon over all but 2 tablespoons of the sour cream. Fold the omelet in half. Stir together the milk and remaining sour cream until smooth. Spoon over the top of the omelet and sprinkle the remaining herbs on top.

Jelly or Jam Omelet

Orange marmalade is delicious in omelets. When using orange marmalade, grate the zest of an orange into the omelet batter before cooking.

1 cup jelly or jam

Warm the jelly or jam in a small pan, stirring constantly until it is melted. Spoon ¾ cup in the center of the omelet before folding in half and spoon the rest on top before serving.

Frittata with Cheese and Crumbs

(five servings)

A frittata is a useful dish for serving many. This frittata is not full of vegetables, like most versions, but suits my early-breakfast sensibilities: rumbled eggs (that's an old term meaning mixed eggs) with buttered crumbs and Cheddar cheese, and a hint of winter savory.

8 tablespoons (1 stick) butter
2 cups fresh, coarse bread crumbs
10 eggs, gently beaten
Salt and pepper to taste

2 teaspoons finely chopped fresh winter savory, or 1 teaspoon crumbled dried winter savory
1 cup grated Cheddar cheese

Preheat the oven to 350°F. Use a 10-inch ovenproof skillet or sauté pan.

Melt 4 tablespoons butter in the skillet over medium heat. Stir in the bread crumbs and cook, stirring often, until they have absorbed the butter and are golden. Remove from the heat and set the crumbs aside. Clean the skillet. In the clean skillet melt the remaining butter over low heat. Sprinkle half the crumbs over the bottom of the skillet. Pour the eggs on top, add salt and pepper sparingly, and then the winter savory. Cook without stirring for a minute or a trifle more (it is important not to overcook), until the bottom has just begun to set. You can tilt the skillet just a little to see. Put the skillet in the oven and bake for just 2 minutes. Sprinkle the cheese and the remaining 1 cup bread crumbs evenly over the top. Bake 1 more minute and remove from the oven. Loosen the edges and slide the frittata onto a large serving plate. This is good hot or cold. Cut into wedges to serve.

Featherbed Eggs

(four servings)

Featherbed Eggs are layers of bread and custard with the addition of cheese or fruit or a favorite something (as long as it isn't too moist or liquid). The joy of this dish is that it must be prepared the day before, or at least six hours before baking, so it is all ready well in advance of need.

6 slices bread, buttered
Salt and pepper to taste
1½ cups grated sharp Cheddar, Gouda, Provolone, Monterey Jack, or any other melting cheese

1½ cups milk
6 eggs, slightly beaten

Arrange the slices of bread in a single layer in a shallow, buttered baking dish. Sprinkle lightly with salt and pepper. Sprinkle the grated cheese evenly over the bread. Combine the milk and eggs, and stir until blended. Pour the milk mixture over the bread and cheese. Cover and refrigerate at least 6 hours, or overnight.

As the dish will be chilled when you are ready to bake it, start it in a cold 350°F oven. Bake for about 1 hour, or until the bread custard is puffy and lightly golden.

Apple Ham Featherbed   Omit the grated cheese and place thin slices of ham over the buttered bread. Pour the custard over. Spread ¼ cup applesauce over each slice of ham; this can be done just before baking, if you wish. Cover and refrigerate at least 6 hours. Bake as directed above.

Fresh Fruit and Cream Cheese Featherbed　Omit the grated cheese and spread each slice of buttered bread with 3 tablespoons softened cream cheese. Pour the custard over, cover, and refrigerate at least 6 hours. Peel and slice any firm, ripe fruit (nectarines, pears, peaches, strawberries). Place a single layer of sliced fruit over the cream cheese. Sprinkle a little sugar over the fruit if it tastes too tart. Bake as directed on page 159.

Oatmeal Soufflé

(four servings)

This is a surprising and good way to eat oatmeal.

1 cup milk	1/2 teaspoon nutmeg
2 tablespoons butter	1/2 teaspoon cinnamon
3/4 cup quick-cooking oatmeal	3 eggs, separated
1/3 cup cream cheese (low-fat)	1/2 cup raisins
1/4 teaspoon salt	1/2 cup chopped walnuts
1/2 cup brown sugar	

Preheat the oven to 325°F. Butter and sugar a 1 1/2-quart soufflé dish or casserole.

Put the milk and butter into a small saucepan and heat until barely boiling. Slowly add the oatmeal, stirring constantly. Cook the oatmeal until thick, stirring often. Remove from the heat and add the cream cheese, salt, sugar, nutmeg, and cinnamon. Stir briskly to blend and smooth the mixture. Beat the 3 yolks slightly and slowly add them to the oatmeal, stirring constantly. Stir in the raisins and walnuts.

Beat the egg whites until they are stiff but still moist. Using a rubber spatula, gently stir and fold the whites into the oatmeal mixture. Don't overfold; fold only until no large lumps of whites remain. Spoon the mixture into the soufflé dish. Bake for 35 to 40 minutes, or until the center still trembles a trifle but most of the soufflé is set. Serve immediately, with cream or warm milk. This soufflé is still tasty when cold and fallen.

Oatmeal Bacon Soufflé Omit the sugar when buttering the soufflé dish. In the recipe, leave out the nutmeg, cinnamon, raisins, and walnuts. Instead, add 1 cup crisp, crumbled bacon, 1¼ teaspoons prepared mustard, and Tabasco to taste.

Lemon Zephyrs

(four servings)

These small free-form soufflés are light as clouds and sweet as the west wind. Breathe carefully or else these fluffy zephyrs may blow right off your plate. Serve with a slice of buttered, toasted pound cake.

4 tablespoons (½ stick) butter	1 teaspoon flour
2 tablespoons milk	2 teaspoons grated lemon rind
7 tablespoons confectioners' sugar	1 cup fresh raspberries
6 egg whites	(or any fresh berries)
¼ teaspoon cream of tartar	Sugar to taste for berries
3 egg yolks	

Preheat the oven to 425°F. Use a shallow (about 2 inches deep) 14-inch oval baking dish; or use a rectangular dish that is an inch shorter. Have a 8- or 9-inch round paper plate at hand.

Combine the butter, milk, and 1 tablespoon confectioners' sugar in the baking dish. Heat the mixture until the butter has melted, stir, and set aside.

Beat the egg whites with the cream of tartar until foamy, then gradually add the remaining 6 tablespoons sugar, and beat until stiff but moist.

Beat the egg yolks thoroughly and add the flour and lemon rind to the yolk mixture. Gently fold the yolk mixture into the beaten whites.

Now you are going to shape the batter into four balls. Using the paper plate as a scoop, pile in a football shape one quarter of the soufflé mixture at the end of the baking dish. Scoop up three more equal portions and drop next to each other. There should be a row of four balls of approximately the same size in the baking dish.

Place the dish in the preheated oven and bake for 5 to 6 minutes, or until the peaks of the soufflés are slightly golden. Sprinkle the berries with sugar if they need some. Remove the soufflés from the oven and sprinkle the berries all over the zephyrs. Bring to the table and serve. Or serve on four individual dessert plates, with a little of the sauce from the bottom of the baking dish spooned over each serving.

Fruit Fixing

One of the reasons I love this subject of breakfast has to do with its utter simplicity—what could be simpler than ripe, fresh fruit? I had a magazine assignment a few years ago that required me to come up with some recipes for tropical fruits—mango, papaya, pineapple, banana. I worked very hard for several weeks and when I got finished with every variation I could think of—and there were lots of them—the fact was that every one of those fruits was best when it was left alone.

When people see bowls of fruit, they think they're just for decoration and don't reach for the fruit. One thing that will encourage your friends or your family to think of fruit as ready to eat and not just something to look at is to put fruit knives and a fork in the bowl. Or put the fruit in bowls with lots of ice and water as another inviting way of saying, "This is something to eat." Keeping a pair of scissors nearby for grapes is a nice touch.

For the sake of demonstrating our desire to please, it is sometimes nice to carve, poach, bake, or ice fresh fruits and berries. The recipes in this chapter with these little extra preparations have not robbed nature of the perfect essence of the fruit.

Simple Ways of Fixing Fruit

Inside-out Mango   I love mangoes — they taste cloudlike, sort of like peaches and ginger. Hold the mango end-up on a board. Using a paring knife, cut as close as possible on either side of the long, flat pit (the mango pit is shaped like a cuttlebone). This will give two shallow halves of mango. Hold one half in the palm of your hand and with the knife cut a pattern like tic-tac-toe squares on the flesh without cutting through the skin. Push the skin-side center of the half upward, as if to turn inside out, so the cut squares protrude. The mango will look quite tailored this way and it will be much easier to eat. Eating a mango left on the pit is best done over the kitchen sink.

Apples   Serve apple slices with walnut halves. Apple slices may be held in salted water — 1 tablespoon salt to 1 quart water. Rinse before serving and the salt disappears. This salted water keeps pears from discoloring, too.

Dates and Figs   Dates and figs are both luscious stuffed with Breakfast Cheese (see page 286) and eaten with walnuts on the side.

Oranges and Grapefruit   Removing sections is a nice gesture. Cut the skin away from the fruit. It is easy to hold the fruit upright on a board and cut away the skin in large strips from the blossom end to the stem end. Cut off any white pith. Cut each section of flesh away from the dividing membranes, so only clean citrus sections are collected.

Pineapple   Cut off the large leafy top. Cut round slices about 1 inch thick and then cut the skin and eyes off each slice. Cut the center core out. Serve the clean slice with raspberry jam or a little coconut.

Grapes   I love the Italian custom of serving bunches of grapes in a bowl of ice and water.

Berries   Strawberries in a ring around some Breakfast Cheese (see page 286) make a lovely presentation. Or serve them with a wedge of lemon and bowls of different kinds of sugar. Strawberries and blueberries are wonderful mixed with finely chopped crystallized ginger, sprinkled with brown sugar, and served with sour cream.

Persimmons   An old California recipe for persimmons is to freeze them, slice them, sprinkle them with brown sugar, and serve with yogurt. Sliced persimmons and grapefruit sections make a fine compote.

Papaya   Papaya becomes a beguiling fruit with a few crunchy, peppery papaya seeds and a little lime juice sprinkled over it. Cut a papaya in half and seed it. Save 1 tablespoon of the seeds, rinse them, and sprinkle over the fruit. Squeeze the juice of half a lime over the top.

Applesauce

(three cups)

I take applesauce so much for granted that I almost left out this recipe. But I had to put it in because it's such a good companion to so many breakfast dishes.

4 large, firm green apples, peeled,
   cored, and cut into eighths
½ cup water

Sugar to taste
3 tablespoons lemon juice

Put the apples and water into a sauté pan. Turn heat to medium and cook, stirring often, until the apples become tender, about 5 or 6 minutes. Add sugar and lemon juice and stir to blend well. Cook another 1 or 2 minutes. Remove from heat and mash with a fork.

Baked Apples

(four servings)

To my mind, the humble, homey baked apple, done properly, is equal to, if not better than, the fanciest pastry.

4 firm, ripe apples
   (pippins or Granny Smiths)
⅓ cup sugar
½ cup water

⅛ teaspoon salt
Zest of 1 lemon, cut into large
   strips

Peel the top third of the apples and core.

Put the sugar, water, salt, and lemon zest in a small pan, bring to a boil, stir, and remove from the heat.

Set the apples upright in a baking dish and pour the syrup over. Cover (use foil if there is no lid that fits) and bake in a preheated 350°F oven for 30 minutes, or until the apples are easily pierced with the tip of a knife. Spoon some of the syrup over the apples and sprinkle a little sugar over the top. You may put them under the broiler for 2 to 3 minutes to brown. Serve warm with cream.

Fried Apple Rings

(eight rings)

Has America forgotten how good apple rings taste, cooked golden with bacon or ham drippings, covered with a little sugar glaze, and served next to bacon or a bit of ham? Apple rings made in this way are also quite good put into a bowl of hot oatmeal, mashed slightly, and covered with milk or cream.

2 tablespoons bacon or ham fat, or butter

2 firm apples, cored, sliced into rings ¼ to ½ inch thick (each apple should yield 4 rings)

⅓ cup sugar, or to taste

Put the fat into a large skillet that will hold 8 apple rings in a single layer. Heat the fat to medium hot, add the rings, and cook for 2 minutes. Sprinkle the sugar over the rings and turn over. Cook for another minute or two, or until the sugar has melted and the apple rings are golden on both sides. Serve hot.

Cranberry Poached Apples

(six small apples)

These apples are a pretty pink and have a slight tartness from the cranberry juice. The fig filling is a nice bonus. They can be prepared the night before.

6 small apples (preferably about
   the size of a peach)
3 cups cranberry juice
1/2 cup sugar
1 small lemon, cut into pieces,
   seeds removed, and ground

3/4 cup figs, chopped fine
2 tablespoons brown sugar
1/4 cup finely chopped walnuts
2 tablespoons lemon juice

Peel the apples and core three quarters of the way to the base. Put the cranberry juice, sugar, and ground lemon into a saucepan large enough to hold the apples in one layer. Bring to a boil, stir, and add the apples to the pan. Add enough water so the liquid comes halfway up the sides of the apples. Cover the pan and bring to a simmer. Uncover and spoon the poaching liquid all over the apples every few minutes, and turn them around gently in the liquid so they are coated often. Depending on the size of the apples, they should simmer 10 to 20 minutes to become tender. Be careful not to cook them to the point where they are falling apart. When the apples are tender, remove the pan from the heat and let them cool in the poaching liquid.

In a small bowl, mix the figs, brown sugar, walnuts, and lemon juice. When the apples are cool, stuff the cored cavities with the fig mixture. Put them in a bowl, taste the liquid, and stir in more sugar or lemon juice as needed. Pour 1 1/2 cups of the liquid over the apples and refrigerate until needed.

Baked Stuffed Pears

(four servings)

This recipe makes a lovely dish. The pears keep their natural good flavor, and the filling adds a special touch.

4 pears, ripe and firm
¼ cup raisins
3 tablespoons chopped walnuts
2½ tablespoons sugar

1 tablespoon lemon juice
¼ cup water
¼ cup light corn syrup

Peel the pears, leaving the stems on. Core the pears on the blossom end (the bottom).

Combine the raisins, walnuts, sugar, and lemon juice in a small bowl, and mix well. Fill the cavity of each pear, dividing the filling equally. Place the pears upright in a deep baking dish, preferably with a cover. Mix together the water and corn syrup and pour into the baking dish. Cover the dish with its lid (or foil) and bake in a preheated 350°F oven for about 1 hour and 15 minutes, or until the pears are easily pierced with a fork. Serve warm or cold with some of the syrup spooned over each pear.

Fresh Orange with Marmalade

(four servings)

A perfect example of a simple dish that is absolutely terrific.

4 oranges, peeled and sectioned
½ cup orange marmalade
   (use less if very sweet)

Place the orange sections in a glass dish. Add the marmalade to the orange sections, refrigerate, and stir to blend after an hour or so. The juice of the oranges will have partially liquefied the marmalade. Refrigerate until *very* cold. I sometimes put this into the freezer for an hour or more before serving to get the mixture quite icy.

Fresh Lemon Juice Ice

(about five cups)

1½ cups sugar
4 cups boiling water

¾ cup freshly squeezed lemon juice
1 tablespoon grated lemon zest

Put the sugar in a bowl and pour the boiling water over. Stir until the sugar dissolves. Cool and add the lemon juice and zest. Freeze as directed for Fresh Grapefruit Juice Ice (following recipe).

Fresh Grapefruit Juice Ice

(about three cups)

This ice is wonderful with ham and hot biscuits. Somehow the icy and slushy grapefruit juice gives an extra sparkle to freshly squeezed juice. Good as a breakfast starter with Gingersnaps (see page 238).

¾ to 1 cup sugar (depending on tartness of grapefruit juice)
½ cup water

3 cups freshly squeezed grapefruit juice

Combine the sugar and water in a saucepan and boil until the sugar is dissolved, about 1 minute. Cool, and stir in the grapefruit juice. Pour into ice cube trays (the small cubed trays are ideal because you can turn out a small dish of cubes for each serving). Or pour the juice mixture into a bowl, cover, and freeze. Remember to soften the ice a trifle so you can serve it easily if you are not freezing it in the tiny cubed ice trays. Serve in little glasses or bowls.

Fresh Orange Juice Ice Substitute orange juice for grapefruit juice, reduce the amount of sugar to ⅓ cup or less, and proceed as directed above.

Rhubarb with English Custard

(four servings)

Mary Hamblit, of Portland, Oregon, served this to me long ago, and it is wonderful. Don't overcook the rhubarb.

1 pound rhubarb, ends trimmed
and cut into 1/2-inch pieces
(about 4 cups)
About 1 1/3 cups water
3/4 cup sugar

A 1/2-inch-thick slice fresh
gingerroot
2 cups English Custard
(see page 283)

Put the rhubarb into a sauté pan that has a lid. Add 1 cup water and cook, covered, over medium heat for 4 to 5 minutes, just until the rhubarb is barely tender (watch the cooking carefully so the rhubarb doesn't turn to mush). Carefully remove the rhubarb from the pan and set aside; discard the water. Put the sugar, 1/3 cup water, and the gingerroot into the sauté pan and heat a minute or two, stirring constantly until the sugar dissolves. Add the rhubarb, stir gently so the rhubarb is covered with syrup, cook 1 minute, and remove from the heat. Let cool. Remove the gingerroot and serve with the English Custard poured over the rhubarb.

Baked Bananas

(six servings)

Why something this easy and good is seldom made is puzzling. Warm baked bananas taste even more like bananas than cold bananas, and somehow anything caramellike is absolute perfection with bananas.

⅓ cup (⅔ stick) butter, melted
3 tablespoons fresh lemon juice
6 firm, ripe bananas, peeled
⅓ cup brown sugar

1 teaspoon cinnamon or
    ground ginger
1 cup grated coconut

Preheat the oven to 375°F.

Spread the melted butter and lemon juice over the bottom of a shallow baking dish that will hold 6 bananas. Stir the butter and lemon juice together until blended. Put the bananas in the dish and turn them until they are well coated with the butter mixture. Put the sugar and cinnamon or ginger in a small bowl and stir with a fork to blend thoroughly. Sprinkle the sugar mixture evenly over the bananas.

Bake the bananas for 18 to 20 minutes, or until the butter bubbles a little. Turn them over once after 10 minutes of baking. Sprinkle the coconut over the bananas about 5 minutes before they finish cooking. Serve warm with a little cream or maple syrup.

Baked Pineapple

(10 servings)

Don't overlook pineapple as a breakfast food; it satisfies that craving for something fresh and tart. Baking a pineapple with a little brown sugar gives it a softer character and a subtle caramel taste.

1 fresh medium pineapple
½ cup brown sugar

Remove the rind and eyes from the pineapple. Cut the fruit into quarters lengthwise and remove the core from each wedge. Cut each quarter in half lengthwise. Sprinkle 1 tablespoon brown sugar over each slice. Place the slices on a baking sheet and bake for 30 minutes in a preheated 325°F oven. Serve warm.

Green Mango Fool

(about 2½ cups)

No fooling, this is a fabulous dish and an indispensable topping for Ginger Pancakes (see page 117).

2 green (unripe) mangoes
   (very firm and hard), peeled,
   cut from seed, and diced
⅓ cup sugar (or more if the
   fruit is very tart)

⅓ cup water
1 cup heavy cream
1½ tablespoons nonfat dry milk

Put the diced mangoes in a saucepan and add the sugar and water. Cook over medium heat, stirring often, for about 10 minutes, or until the fruit is soft. Taste and add more sugar if the fruit is too tart. Remove from heat and mash the mango with a fork until it is a coarse purée. If there is extra liquid, drain some away—this should have the texture of applesauce. Cool before adding to the cream.

Put the heavy cream and nonfat dry milk in a bowl and whip until the cream holds firm peaks. (Adding nonfat dry milk is a tip from Abby Mandel on how to stabilize whipped cream.) Gently stir the mango purée into the whipped cream. Spoon a little mound on top of each ginger pancake. If you don't use all the mango fool, freeze it—it makes delicious ice cream.

Ballymaloe Baked Breakfast Fruit

(eight servings)

This good fruit recipe was given to me by Darina Allen, a lovely young Irish woman who directs the Ballymaloe Cooking School in County Cork, Ireland, with her mother-in-law, Myrtle Allen.

1 cup dried prunes, pitted	½ cup water
1 cup dried apricots	Grated zest of ½ lemon
⅓ cup raisins	2 tablespoons butter
3 bananas, sliced thick	1 cup orange juice
2 tablespoons honey	

Put the prunes and the apricots in a bowl and cover with hot water. Soak overnight.

Drain, and put the prunes, apricots, raisins, and bananas in a baking dish. Dissolve the honey in the water. Sprinkle the lemon zest over the fruit and then pour the honey syrup over. Dot with the butter.

Bake in a preheated 350°F oven for about 35 minutes. Add the orange juice and continue to bake long enough for the orange juice to get hot, about 5 more minutes. Serve warm. It is nice with light cream poured over.

To serve cold: Follow the preceding directions, but omit the bananas and orange juice. Reserve ¾ cup of the water that the fruit soaked in, add it to the honey, and pour it over the fruit. Put into a baking dish, omit the butter, and bake as directed. Cool and refrigerate. Just before serving, add a little fresh orange juice and some sliced bananas. This keeps for about 10 days in the refrigerator.

Pink Grapefruit Apple Dish

(six servings)

The combination of grapefruit and apple is surprisingly right. The tart grapefruit keeps the apple crisp and white, and the bit of fresh mint makes the dish sparkle. Gingersnaps (see page 238) should be served with this.

4 pink grapefruit
4 sweet, firm apples

1 teaspoon finely chopped
fresh mint

Peel the grapefruit and remove the sections from the white pith and membrane. Put the sections in a bowl. Peel and core the apples and slice into thin wedges. Add the apple immediately to the grapefruit and gently stir so the apple slices are coated with the acid grapefruit juice. If there is not enough liquid to cover, boil ½ cup water with ¼ cup sugar, cool a little, and add to the fruit. Chill, and add the fresh mint.

Fresh Orange and Cranberry Compote

(six servings)

Why limit the use of cranberries to a relish for Thanksgiving turkey when it can be eaten with corn muffins year round? And if you yearn for a sharp, tasty complement to a plateful of Bannocks (see page 57), nothing could be better than this compote.

1½ cups fresh cranberries
⅓ cup sugar
¼ cup water

4 juice oranges, peeled, sliced
into rounds, and seeded

Put the cranberries in a small skillet and sprinkle the sugar over them. Add the water and cook over low heat, stirring often. Cook until the sugar has dissolved and the cranberries have popped, about 3 or 4 minutes. Remove the skillet from the heat and add the orange slices. Gently stir, spooning the cranberry juice over the slices until well saturated. Serve warm or chilled.

Potatoes

Rough and Ready Potatoes
Oven Fries
Hash Brown Potatoes
Raw Potato Pancakes
Potato Bacon Pie
   Cottage Cheese Potato Bacon Pie
Potato Apple Fry
Potato Custard
Creek Bank Potatoes

The potato is the strong, silent type, and because it is not assertive, it is the most popular breakfast vegetable. There is no food quite like the potato. We take them for granted, like an old friend, and seldom stop to think of their virtues: they are always available, cheap, nutritious, digestible. And like best friends, you can always count on them. Potatoes give substance to a meal and they have a wholesome gentle taste and down-to-earth goodness.

I happen to love potatoes and eggs; I could eat them every day of the week. Somehow they belong together, especially potatoes with eggs fried sunny-side-up (potatoes mop up that nice yolk better than toast).

Once in a blue moon, you may notice a greenish tinge on the surface of a potato. This indicates the presence of some natural poisons that form near the surface when the potato is about to sprout, so be sure to cut this all away.

Rough and Ready Potatoes

(two servings)

In under ten minutes you can have a batch of dark brown Rough and Ready Potatoes so delicious that you will want to make them every time you fry an egg.

1 large russet potato
1 tablespoon bacon fat or
   shortening

Salt and pepper to taste

Don't peel the potato but scrub it well; cut into cubes about ½ inch square. Melt the fat in a skillet. When the fat is very hot, stand back and add the potatoes. Salt and pepper liberally. Let the potato cubes fry for about 4 minutes, turn them over with a spatula, and salt and pepper again. Cook the potatoes another 3 minutes, until they are dark and brown. Serve hot.

Oven Fries

(three servings)

Oven fries are like French fries: they are identically shaped, they taste delicious, but they aren't deep fried.

2 russet potatoes, peeled
¼ cup vegetable oil

Salt and lots of pepper

Preheat the oven to 425°F.

Cut the potatoes into pieces ½ inch wide and about 3½ inches long. Pour the oil into a 10-inch pie pan or square pan. Put the pieces of potato in the pan and turn them over on all sides to completely coat with a film of oil. Salt and pepper liberally. Put the potatoes in the oven and set the timer for 15 minutes. When the timer goes off, turn the potatoes over and add salt and pepper. Set the timer again for 10 minutes, then pour off any liquid in the pan and turn the potatoes for the last time. Bake for another 15 minutes and they will be golden around the edges. Remove from the oven and serve hot.

Hash Brown Potatoes

(three servings)

Hash browns are an American native. Every diner, coffee shop, and truck stop in the country serves these crisp, browned potatoes with eggs. They give a fine balance and roughness to fried or scrambled eggs. Adding cream is optional; they will still be crisp, but slightly more moist inside.

3 tablespoons bacon fat, oil,
or shortening
3 cups grated potatoes,
raw or cooked

Salt and lots of pepper
Optional: ⅓ cup heavy cream

Heat the fat in a large skillet. Spread the potatoes in a layer, pressing down with a spatula. Add salt and pepper to taste. Cook over medium heat for 6 or 7 minutes. With the edge of the spatula, cut the circle of potatoes down the middle. Turn each half over and, if using cream, pour it evenly over the potatoes. Sprinkle again with salt and pepper. Cook another 6 or 7 minutes, or until the potatoes are crisp and brown on the bottom. Serve hot.

Raw Potato Pancakes

(eight 3½-inch pancakes)

Potato pancakes are crisp and brown on the outside, and the inside has the nice, slightly biting flavor of fresh potato. Served two or three per person with hot homemade Applesauce (see page 168) and a couple of thick slices of bacon with a little maple syrup over, these make a fine winter breakfast. Sour cream or cottage cheese beaten until smooth is also good on these pancakes. Potato pancakes can be made in quantity and frozen. To cook, heat a little fat in a hot griddle or skillet and quickly fry the pancakes on both sides.

2 medium-size russet potatoes, peeled and grated (to make 2 cups)*
⅓ cup heavy cream
4 tablespoons clarified butter; or vegetable shortening or bacon fat, melted; or vegetable oil

Salt to taste
Lots of coarsely ground black pepper

*NOTE: If you wish to do this in advance, put the grated potatoes in cold salted water to cover for up to 2 hours. Drain and pat dry on paper towels before using.

Just before you are ready to fry the pancakes, put the grated potatoes in a bowl and stir in the cream. Heat the fat until sizzling hot in a large skillet. Have some paper towels at hand. Don't worry if the potatoes become slightly pink while you are waiting for the fat to heat.

When the skillet is ready, measure out about ¼ cup potato and drop into the skillet. Stand back a little, as the cream tends to spatter when it meets the hot fat. Press the mound of potato down with a spatula to flatten and shape into a round pancake. Sprinkle the top lightly with salt and liberally with pepper. Cook until the edges are golden brown. Turn over and cook the other side until crisp and brown. Pat each pancake on the paper towels to get rid of excess fat, and keep them hot on a plate in a 250°F oven — or better yet, serve immediately. If needed for future use, pat them dry of excess fat, wrap well, and freeze.

Potato Bacon Pie

(one 8-inch pie)

The next time you bake or boil potatoes, make extra so that you will have enough left over to make this pie. Potato Bacon Pie has a nice texture since the cooked potato is grated or mashed into bits rather than puréed or whipped. Serve a wedge of this pie with eggs. Potato Bacon Pie can be prepared in advance, kept refrigerated overnight, and baked in the morning.

4 cups cooked potato, grated or mashed into bits	Salt to taste
Lots of coarsely ground black pepper	½ cup milk
	12 slices bacon, fried, patted dry of fat, and crumbled

Preheat the oven to 350°F. Butter an 8-inch pie pan.

Put the potato, pepper, salt, milk, and bacon in a bowl, and mix well. Spread the potato mixture evenly into the pie pan. Bake for about 40 minutes, or until the top has become lightly browned.

Cottage Cheese Potato Bacon Pie   Substitute 1½ cups cottage cheese for 1½ cups of the cooked potato. Proceed as directed above.

Potato Apple Fry

(six servings)

This combination looks appealing, and tastes good for breakfast. The apples should be as tart as possible – dousing with lemon juice helps. Sour cream served on the side brings out the best of the sharp new potato and tart apple tastes.

3 firm, tart apples (pippin or Granny Smith)	2 tablespoons vegetable oil
5 tablespoons fresh lemon juice	6 medium-size new red potatoes
4 tablespoons (½ stick) butter	Salt to taste
	Sour cream

Peel and core the apples, and slice them ⅛ inch thick. Put the apple slices in a shallow bowl and sprinkle the lemon juice all over. Toss until the lemon juice penetrates each slice.

Put the butter and oil in a large skillet that has a lid. Leave over very low heat while preparing the potatoes. Don't peel the potatoes, just scrub and then slice them ⅛ inch thick. Turn the heat up to medium high and spread the potato slices evenly over the skillet. Salt to taste. Cook the slices until lightly browned, then turn them over to lightly brown the other side.

Drain the apple slices of lemon juice and add to the potatoes in the skillet, tossing to mix. Cover and cook over high heat for a minute or two. Uncover, and cook another 2 minutes, turning once or twice. Serve hot with sour cream.

Potato Custard

(three servings)

This is a dish fit for the fussiest eater. Potatoes are sliced thin, lightly salted and generously peppered, covered with eggs and milk and bits of butter, and baked into a congenial custard. It is nice to add some crumbled cooked sausage, ham, or bacon, if you have some on hand.

4 tablespoons (½ stick) butter (plus 1 tablespoon for buttering the dish)	Salt and pepper to taste 2 eggs ½ cup milk
2 medium-size baking potatoes	

Preheat the oven to 350°F. Lavishly butter a shallow 1-quart baking dish.

Peel the potatoes and slice very thin. Spread a layer of potatoes over the baking dish in a single layer, sprinkle with salt and liberally with pepper, and dot a tablespoon or two of butter over the potatoes. Repeat layering, salting and peppering, and buttering, until all the potatoes are used.

Beat the eggs and milk together until mixed. Pour over the potatoes. Bake for 30 to 40 minutes, or until the potatoes are just tender when pierced with a knife. Serve hot.

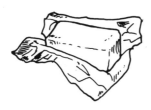

Creek Bank Potatoes

(four servings)

This recipe is for the kind of potatoes you would get on a fishing trip — cooked up at dawn in a skillet on a creek bank, and there waiting for you whether you caught anything or not. Just the thing you would want to eat on a cold morning when you are feeling lean.

4 russet potatoes	2 tablespoons vegetable oil
1 large onion	2 tablespoons bacon fat
6 tablespoons (¾ stick) butter, melted	Salt and lots of pepper

Don't peel the potatoes. Scrub and cut them into quarters lengthwise; then slice crosswise into ⅜-inch pieces. Rinse in cold water. Coarsely chop the onion. Mix the butter, vegetable oil, and bacon fat in a bowl. Add the potatoes and onion and toss with salt to taste and coarsely ground pepper. Throw the potatoes into the skillet over medium-high heat and shake to spread them evenly. Cover the skillet and cook over medium heat 40 minutes, shaking the pan occasionally.

Variation If you're not on a creek bank, these potatoes are wonderful done in the oven. You will need a 10- or 11-inch ovenproof skillet; if yours has a handle that is not ovenproof, cover with several layers of foil. Put all the ingredients into the skillet, toss together, and put the skillet into a preheated 425°F oven. The potatoes will take approximately 20 minutes to bake.

Meat and Fish

Breakfast Steak
Creamed Chipped Beef with Mushrooms
Corned Beef Hash
Pork Tenderloin with Biscuits and Gravy
Breakfast Sausage
Ham and Bacon
  Ruffled Ham
  Ham Loaf
  Chipped Ham with Dried Apricots
Bacon
Fresh Fish
Trout Fried with Oatmeal
Fish Hash
Smoked and Salted Fish
Red Flannel Fish Hash
Kedgeree
Salt Cod Cakes
Salt Cod Potato Breakfast

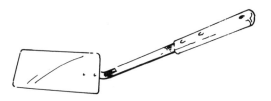

I hardly ever think of meat as the most important part of a breakfast menu, and never as the only dish. It should be considered more as an accompaniment to the main ingredients of breakfast—grains, dairy products, fruit, and sometimes eggs. I only serve meat in very, very small amounts, but that little bit can make everything else taste better.

To Mark Twain, and to many Americans a hundred years ago, breakfast meant "a mighty porterhouse steak an inch and a half thick, hot and sputtering from the griddle; dusted with fragrant pepper; enriched with little melting bits of butter...; the precious juices of the meat trickling out and joining the gravy, archipelagoed with mushrooms;...and a great cup of American homemade coffee... some smoking-hot biscuits, a plate of hot buckwheat cakes, with transparent syrup..." This *sounds* wonderful, but the small Breakfast Steak following is more appetizing to me. Big portions of ham, bacon, and sausage are all well and good for lumberjacks, but not for most everyday appetites. And after all, who wants to cook dinner for breakfast? And who can afford to?

Fresh fish, on the other hand, has a certain delicacy and lightness that occasionally seems right for breakfast. Simply broiled or pan fried, fish can be a refreshing high-protein alternative to high-fat meats like ham and bacon. Cured fish—salted, dried, or smoked—is practically a stranger to the American breakfast table. Try out the cured fish recipes in this chapter and you may become a convert.

Breakfast Steak

Breakfast steaks are small tenderloins, about 1/4 inch thick, weighing about 3 ounces. If you want to have a well-seared outside and a raw inside, the only way to do it is to start with a frozen steak. Use a heavy skillet, and if you are not in a hurry, trim about 1 tablespoon of fat off the steak and let it slowly melt in the skillet over medium-low heat: I take the back of a spoon, and as the skillet heats up I press down on the fat until the skillet is lubricated. When the skillet is filmed with fat, turn the heat to high and let the skillet get super hot. Put the steak or steaks in the skillet, salt and pepper liberally, and pan fry for about 1 minute on each side.

Creamed Chipped Beef with Mushrooms

(four servings)

You might be disdainful of creamed dishes and I wouldn't blame you, having been served lots of pasty cream sauce over the years (and over the toast). But this dish, with a proper cream sauce, will change your mind. It is very nice over a crisp waffle or whole wheat toast.

2 1/2 ounces sliced dried beef,
   rinsed under cold water
   if too salty
5 tablespoons butter
1 1/2 cups cleaned and sliced fresh
   mushrooms

3 tablespoons flour
2 1/2 cups milk
Salt and pepper to taste

Shred the beef into a bowl by tearing the slices into bits.

Melt 2 tablespoons butter in a skillet over medium heat. Add the mushrooms and cook for a minute, stirring, just until they change color a little. Remove the mushrooms with a slotted spoon to the bowl containing the beef.

Melt the remaining 3 tablespoons butter in the skillet over medium heat. Add the flour and cook, stirring constantly, for about 2 minutes. Still stirring, slowly add the milk. Add the salt and pepper. Stir and cook for at least 5 minutes, until the sauce has thickened. Stir in the beef and mushrooms, cook another 10 seconds, remove from the heat, and serve.

Corned Beef Hash

(four servings)

Patience is the essential ingredient for making good hash. Next, you will need lots of pepper and some salt. If you insist on using it, serve with warm chili sauce. This recipe makes a darn good hash.

4 cups cooked and finely diced corned beef	Lots of pepper
	Salt to taste
3 cups cooked and finely diced potatoes	3 tablespoons butter
	2 tablespoons oil
1 cup grated or finely chopped onion	1/2 cup heavy cream

Put the corned beef, potatoes, and onion in a large bowl. Sprinkle with pepper and salt. Toss and mix the ingredients well.

Heat the butter and oil in a large skillet that has a cover. Add the hash and spread over the bottom of the skillet. Press the hash down with a spatula. Pour the cream evenly over the hash. Cover and cook over medium-low heat for about 10 minutes—don't hurry this. Uncover and check the bottom of the hash to see how brown it is getting—it will take at least 10 minutes to get lightly browned if the heat is moderately low. Turn the heat to high and cook, uncovered, for 5 minutes more. Invert the hash onto a warm plate and serve.

Pork Tenderloin with Biscuits and Gravy

(four servings)

If you are going to be working hard physically, this farm breakfast will fortify you and keep your strength up the whole morning. Hot home-made Applesauce (see page 168) is a nice accompaniment.

Twelve ¾-inch-thick pork tender-
   loin pieces (about 2 inches in
   diameter)
	Gravy

	¼ cup bacon fat
	¼ cup all-purpose flour
½ cup all-purpose flour	Salt and pepper to taste
Salt and pepper to taste	2 cups half-and-half
3 tablespoons bacon fat	

Cream Biscuits (see page 48)

Trim any thick pieces of fat from the edges of the tenderloin, but leave a little. Blend together the flour, salt, and pepper on a piece of waxed paper. Dredge each round of pork in the seasoned flour. Shake to remove any excess flour and place on a piece of waxed paper.

Melt the 3 tablespoons bacon fat in a 10-inch skillet. When the fat is hot, place the pork pieces in a single layer in the skillet. Brown quickly on each side, lower the heat, and let the pork cook gently for about 5 minutes, or until cooked through. Remove the meat to a heated plate, and cover to keep warm while making the gravy.

To make the gravy, add the ¼ cup bacon fat to the fat left in the skillet that cooked the pork pieces. With a spatula, scrape up all the bits from the bottom of the pan to include in the gravy. Add the flour, salt, and pepper, and over medium heat stir slowly but constantly, cooking the roux until the flour is a nut-brown color. Slowly add the half-and-half, still stirring constantly, and cook over medium-low heat until the gravy is smooth and thickened.

Provide 3 tenderloin pieces for each serving, with biscuits on the side. Encourage everyone to split the biscuits and spoon gravy over them and the pork.

Breakfast Sausage

(sixteen 3-inch links or twelve patties)

The following recipe may be made into patties or into sausage links. If you choose to make the links (stuffing the sausage into casing) you will need three hands, so enlist the aid of some patient soul in the house. Sausage links make a juicier sausage when cooked than the patty, but I think both are splendid if some basic directions are followed. It is very important to have one-third fat to two-thirds pork. If you buy pork butt from a supermarket you will have ample fat. Ask the butcher to grind the pork butt or do it yourself. (It should be ground coarse or "chili-grind.") If the pork is too lean to supply the necessary proportion of one-third fat, ask to buy additional pork fat and have it coarsely ground in with the pork butt meat. If you are grinding your meat at home, have the meat well chilled so the fat doesn't soften and blend into the meat — chilling will help keep the fat more intact during the grinding and mixing.

2 pounds pork butt (1/3 fat to 2/3 pork), ground coarse or "chili-grind," chilled
1½ teaspoons freshly ground pepper
1¼ teaspoons salt

1½ tablespoons minced fresh sage, or 2½ teaspoons crumbled dried sage
2 teaspoons minced fresh thyme, or 1 teaspoon crumbled dried thyme

Combine the ground pork, pepper, salt, sage, and thyme in a large mixing bowl. Thoroughly mix the ingredients, but do it as gently as possible so the mixture doesn't become "creamy." This will not be a problem if the meat is chilled.

Stuffing casing to make links

Sausage casing may be either plastic or natural hog casing. The natural is much superior, so try using it. Many butcher shops carry hog casing—it comes in irregular lengths in small cartons and is packed in salt. It will keep for many months in the refrigerator if you keep it well packed in salt. Take about 5 feet of casing and soak it in water for about an hour before using. Rinse well to remove the excess salt.

Use a 12- or 16-inch pastry bag fitted with a ½-inch tube. Open the end of the sausage casing and slip it up onto the tube fitting. Push all of the casing up onto the tube fitting so it is bunched up, leaving a tail about 2 inches long. Knot the little piece of casing tail. Fill the bag with sausage, leaving 3 inches of unfilled bag at the top so you can twist the bag and push the sausage through the tube opening. Here is the point where you will need an extra hand. Have someone firmly hold the bunched-up casing on the tube while you twist the top of the bag, then push the sausage through into the casing. As the sausage fills the casing to the length you want, give the casing a couple of turns, which will complete each link as it is filled. Proceed until you have used up all the sausage meat.

Just before frying the sausage, prick each link with the point of a sharp knife in several places so the fat can escape during cooking. Fry the sausage over medium-low heat, covered for 5 minutes; then cook uncovered, turning once or twice, to brown for about 5 minutes more.

Sausage Patties

If the sausage is too sticky to handle, wet your hands with cold water. For each patty, use about ½ cup sausage and pat into a round, flat disk. Cook over high heat for about 2 minutes on each side to brown, and then lower the heat and finish cooking for about another 2 minutes. Pat dry of excess fat on paper towels and serve hot.

Sausage Rolls This is a fine way to prepare sausage for lots of people. Preheat the oven to 400°F. Cut four strips of parchment paper 12 inches long and 5 inches wide. Butter each piece on one side. Divide the sausage mixture into 4 equal parts. Lightly flour your hands and roll and pat each piece into a 12-inch roll. Place each roll on a piece of buttered parchment and roll the parchment around it. Place each roll, loose side down, on a baking sheet. Bake the rolls for about 10 minutes. Unwrap and cut each roll into the desired size for serving.

HAM AND BACON

In the past, pork was salt-cured, dried, and sometimes smoked to preserve it. Our taste for cured ham and bacon has outlasted necessity, and most of the ham and bacon sold today is salted just for flavor. The curing process used to take a year or more. Today, bacon and ham are injected with brine and steam-smoked, all in less than a day.

Almost all supermarket hams are precooked and ready to eat. Many of them have the bone removed, and some are even presliced. All of these hams lack the complex character of hams cured the old-fashioned way. I think that a ham without its bone has lost its soul—it is bland and soft.

One of the best buys in cured pork is smoked picnic shoulder. (A ham is the hind leg of a pig; the picnic shoulder is the fore leg.) Smoked picnic shoulders are less expensive than ham, and they have a deep, smoky flavor—a world apart from canned hams.

It is still possible to buy country ham cured the same way hams have been cured for hundreds of years. Country hams will differ depending on the breed of pig, its age, and diet (the best Italian hams are supposed to be fed on chestnuts and cheese whey; some Southern pigs are still fed on peanuts). The curing process varies, too: the hams may be dry- or brine-cured and the cure may include sugar, maple sugar, molasses, pepper or other spices, and nitrite. And hams are smoked for different lengths of time, with different kinds of fuel—corncobs, apple, hickory, or sassafras, to name a few. Differences in climate, altitude, and the amount of time the ham is allowed to age will also alter the taste of a ham. Some hams are still aged for over a year. Here is a list of just a few mail-order sources of country hams. There are many more, and your taste will have to guide you to the ham you like best.

Col. Bill Newsom's Kentucky Country Hams
127 North Highland Avenue
Princeton, KY 42445
(502) 365-2482

Comstock Farms
Church Street
Barton, VT 05822
(802) 525-3444

Lawrence's Smoke House
R.R. 1, Box 28
Newfane, VT 05345
(802) 365-7751

Ozark Mountain Smokehouse
P.O. Box 37
Farmington, AR 72730
(800) 643-3437

Smithfield Ham and Products Company
P.O. Box 487
Smithfield, VA 23430
(804) 357-2121

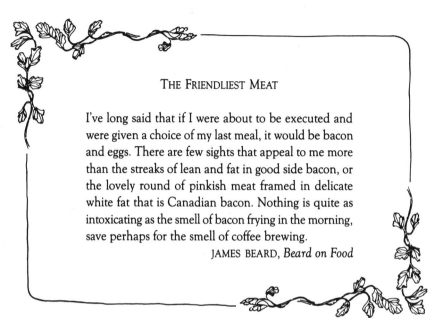

THE FRIENDLIEST MEAT

I've long said that if I were about to be executed and were given a choice of my last meal, it would be bacon and eggs. There are few sights that appeal to me more than the streaks of lean and fat in good side bacon, or the lovely round of pinkish meat framed in delicate white fat that is Canadian bacon. Nothing is quite as intoxicating as the smell of bacon frying in the morning, save perhaps for the smell of coffee brewing.

JAMES BEARD, *Beard on Food*

Ruffled Ham

This is an attractive and appetizing way to serve just a little bit of ham without feeling ungenerous. For some of us who are watching our weight, the flavor of even a little ham with eggs or whatever is satisfying. A couple of crinkled-up slices of paper-thin Ruffled Ham per serving will fill the bill. The ham can be "ruffling" while you cook eggs or something else to serve with it.

Buy a small piece of your favorite kind of ham and have it sliced paper-thin. Buying ham in a delicatessen, where slicing to order is the usual practice, can save you from looking for an accommodating butcher.

Preheat the oven to 350°F. For each serving, separate two slices of ham and, one at a time, crumple up the slices in your hand. Put them both in an ovenproof custard cup or a small bowl. Put the cup (or as many cups as there are servings) into the oven and allow to heat through, about 10 minutes. Turn each serving out onto a plate and serve.

Ham Loaf

(four servings)

This is extremely good, hot or cold: it sets nicely and it slices easily without crumbling. Of course, a good ham loaf depends on good ham—beware those watery canned ones. Serve with warm Raw Apple Muffins (see page 58).

3 cups ground ham	1 whole bay leaf, crumbled
1½ pounds ground pork	1 cup fresh bread crumbs
½ teaspoon coarsely ground pepper	(preferably dark rye bread crumbs)
2 teaspoons finely chopped fresh thyme, or 1 teaspoon crumbled dried thyme	1 egg, lightly beaten
	½ cup milk

Preheat the oven to 350°F. Butter a medium-size loaf pan.

Mix all ingredients together in a bowl, tossing until well combined. Lightly pack into the loaf pan. Bake for 40 to 50 minutes, or until the fat is bubbling around the edges. Remove and pour off any excess fat. Allow to set for 10 to 15 minutes in the pan before turning out. Serve hot or cold.

Chipped Ham with Dried Apricots

(four servings)

Tart and sour flavors have a traditional affinity for pork, ham, and sausages—think of sauerkraut. In this dish, the sour taste of dried apricots goes well with the smoky flavor of ham. Serve this hot, spooned over a crisp waffle, white toast, or rye toast.

1 cup dried apricots
2 cups boiling water
3 tablespoons butter
2 tablespoons flour
3 cups milk
1 teaspoon dry English mustard
  dissolved in 2 tablespoons
  water

Salt to taste (be careful—
  ham is quite salty)
1 cup shredded or coarsely
  chopped cooked ham

Put the dried apricots in a bowl and pour 2 cups boiling water over. Let stand for 15 minutes, until the apricots have softened. Cut them into small pieces and set aside.

Melt the butter in a skillet and stir in the flour. Cook over medium heat, stirring constantly, for 2 minutes. Continuing to stir, slowly add the milk. Add the mustard and salt, and cook the sauce for 5 minutes. Then add the apricots and ham and cook for another minute. Taste, correct seasoning, and serve.

Bacon

Bacon is cured pork belly. Bacon cut from a slab at a deli counter or by a reliable butcher may be better than packaged, presliced supermarket bacon. The taste of old-fashioned cured bacon is so much better that it will spoil you forever. Some of the smokehouses that supply country hams also sell bacon.

To pan-fry bacon, start it in a cold skillet and cook slowly, over medium-low heat, turning over at least once and pouring off excess fat. If you like your bacon slices quite flat, you can weight the bacon down in the skillet with the bottom of another, smaller pan.

To broil bacon, place the slices on the rack of a broiling pan or roasting pan with a little water in it. Put the pan about 4 inches from the broiling unit. Turn the slices once, midway through the 3- to 5-minute cooking time.

To bake bacon, place the slices on a rack in a pan and bake in a 400°F oven for 10 to 12 minutes.

Fresh Fish

Fresh fish cooked simply would be good for breakfast—try it lightly floured or cooked in cornmeal, pan fried or broiled, whole or filleted. A good rule of thumb for estimating cooking time, regardless of method or type of fish, is to figure 10 minutes of cooking time per inch of thickness (at the fish's thickest point). Remember that this 10-minute rule is a compromise—it overestimates the time needed to cook a thin piece of fish. The type of fish should be taken into account, too.

Very thin, very delicate fish fillets under 1/2 inch thick are a snap to pan fry. Just cook in a little butter and oil for about 15 to 20 seconds, cover the pan, cook for 15 seconds more, take the lid off, and serve.

Trout Fried with Oatmeal

(four servings)

Rainbow trout is the kind of trout most commonly found in markets. It ranges in weight from 1 to 2 pounds and is 10 to 12 inches long. This delicate white fish is best when very little is done to it other than cooking briefly and serving with lemon. The oatmeal makes a good coating that is mild in taste but lends a nice texture.

1/2 cup milk	4 trout (leave the heads and tails
2/3 cup rolled oats	on, unless you are squeamish)
1/4 cup shortening, or a combina-	Salt and pepper to taste
tion of oil and butter	Lemon wedges

Pour the milk in a large deep plate and spread the oatmeal on a piece of waxed paper. If you want a finer-textured oatmeal than the flakes, whir the rolled oats in a food processor.

Put the shortening in a large skillet and heat it over high heat. Dip each trout in the milk and then in the oatmeal, coating each side completely. Put the trout in the hot shortening and turn the heat down to medium-high. Salt and pepper the trout and cook for 3 to 4 minutes; then turn the trout and cook for 3 to 4 minutes on the other side—don't overcook. Remove from the pan and serve with lemon wedges.

Fish Hash

(four servings)

The goodness of this simple hash depends on good fish and lots of freshly ground pepper.

3 tablespoons bacon fat
3 cups cooked potatoes, peeled
   and cut into small dice
1 teaspoon freshly ground pepper

2 cups cooked, flaked fish
Salt to taste
1/2 cup heavy cream

Melt the bacon fat in a large skillet over high heat. Spread the potatoes evenly over the skillet, sprinkle with the pepper, and reduce heat to medium to cook for 4 to 5 minutes. Spread the fish evenly over the potatoes, pressing down with a spatula, and salt lightly. Drizzle the cream evenly over the hash and let cook another 4 to 5 minutes. Lift the edge of the hash with a spatula and check to see that it is getting nicely browned on the bottom; turn the heat up a trifle if it isn't. Cook until good and brown, turn onto a warm platter, and serve.

Smoked and Salted Fish

When cod and similar fish are preserved by drying they are called stockfish; when preserved by partial drying after being salted they are known as salt cod. Salt cod requires soaking before it can be cooked to reconstitute its flesh and get rid of excessive saltiness.

Haddock is preserved by light salting and smoking. When split and smoked to a golden-yellow, it is called finnan haddie.

To freshen salt cod or salt mackerel, cover the fish with cold water and soak for 8 hours, changing the water at least once. Taste the fish; if it is still too salty, soak in another change of water for another hour or two, or cover with milk and simmer for 5 minutes or so.

To freshen finnan haddie, it is best to soak the fish in cold milk for an hour, drain, and then poach in milk. The milk sweetens the fish and tames its saltiness. The poaching milk can be thickened with flour, cooked, and made into a very tasty sauce.

Red Flannel Fish Hash

(four servings)

Red flannel hash always has beets in it. This dish is especially good with any salted fish – the beets lend a faint sweetness that balances the saltiness. Red Flannel Fish Hash is very tasty and looks inviting with its streaks of red and pink.

1 cup beets, cooked, peeled,
    and diced
2 cups potatoes, cooked and diced
2 cups salted mackerel or cod,
    freshened (see above)
    and flaked

½ teaspoon pepper
3 tablespoons butter
½ cup milk

Put the beets, potatoes, fish, and pepper together in a bowl, and toss to mix.

Melt the butter in a heavy skillet. Spread the hash evenly over the bottom of the skillet and drizzle the milk evenly over the hash. Cook over medium-low heat for about 10 minutes. Watch carefully and lift the edge of the hash with a spatula from time to time to make sure it isn't burning. Turn the hash over – it is easy to turn over one small section at a time. Continue to cook for another 5 minutes. Serve hot.

Kedgeree

(four servings)

Kedgeree is an English breakfast dish that originated in India. We made this dish many times in James Beard's cooking classes and it always met with great approval. The flavors and textures are wonderful: the faintly smoky finnan haddie and the mild spiciness of curry and nutmeg; the chewy basmati rice and the soft finnan haddie. We served this dish on a large platter with scrambled eggs in the center and the kedgeree in a ring around the eggs.

3 hard-boiled eggs, peeled and chopped fine
1½ cups freshened, boned, skinned, and flaked finnan haddie, or any cooked or smoked fish (see page 207)
3 cups cooked rice (try brown basmati rice)
¾ cup heavy cream
1 teaspoon curry powder
½ teaspoon nutmeg
Generous grindings of black pepper
3 tablespoons lemon juice
Salt if needed

Put the eggs, fish, and rice in a large mixing bowl. Toss together lightly to mix. Put the cream in a small saucepan, add the curry powder and nutmeg, and heat, stirring until the spices are blended. Add the cream mixture, pepper, and lemon juice to the rice mixture, and gently toss. Taste for salt and add some if needed (the dish won't need any if the smoked fish is salty). Put the Kedgeree in a casserole and heat in a moderate (325°F) oven only until hot. Serve as described above.

Salt Cod Cakes

(six cakes)

It is a shame that salt cod seems to be fading away on our menus. It has a distinct character which absolutely shines in some dishes. These codfish cakes are a good example—serve them with plenty of lemon wedges and bacon, Crisp Whole Wheat Buns (see page 18), and slices of melon. Soak the salt cod in several changes of cold water for 12 hours. Drain, put in a saucepan, cover with cold water, and add a bay leaf and a little thyme. Bring the water to a bare simmer and let the cod poach for 10 minutes. Drain and proceed with the Salt Cod Cakes.

1 cup flaked salt cod
    (prepared as directed above)
1½ cups mashed potatoes
2 eggs, lightly beaten
1 teaspoon pepper

3 tablespoons milk
¼ cup flour
¼ cup yellow cornmeal
3 tablespoons shortening

Mix the cod, potatoes, eggs, pepper, and milk if needed (add only if the mixture seems too dry to you) in a bowl. Using a large spoon, beat briskly until the mixture is well combined. Divide into 6 equal parts. On a piece of waxed paper combine the flour and cornmeal.

Heat the shortening in a large skillet over medium-high heat. Pat the cod cakes into 4-inch patties. Dredge with the flour and cornmeal. Cook the cakes until brown on each side. Serve hot.

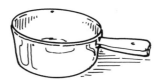

Salt Cod Potato Breakfast

(four servings)

This dish is easily made the night before and popped into the oven in the morning to be heated and served. Salt cod, potato, cream sauce, and crisp crumbs make a breakfast for champions.

4 tablespoons (½ stick) butter
3 tablespoons flour
3 cups milk
¼ teaspoon pepper
2 cups potatoes, cooked and cut
    into small dice

1½ cups salt cod, freshened (see
    page 207), poached, and flaked
3 hard-boiled eggs, diced
Salt to taste
1 cup fresh bread crumbs

Butter a 3-quart casserole.

Melt the 4 tablespoons butter in a heavy-bottomed saucepan and stir in the flour. Cook over medium heat, stirring constantly, for 2 minutes. Slowly add the milk, still stirring, and continue to cook until the mixture thickens. Add the pepper and cook for 3 more minutes, stirring. Remove from the heat and add the potatoes, cod, and hard-boiled eggs. Taste and add salt if needed. Stir gently and spoon the mixture into the casserole. Sprinkle the crumbs evenly over the top. Put in a preheated 350°F oven and bake for 25 minutes; if the dish has been refrigerated, bake for 45 minutes, or until the sauce is bubbling a bit around the edges. Serve hot.

Custards and Puddings

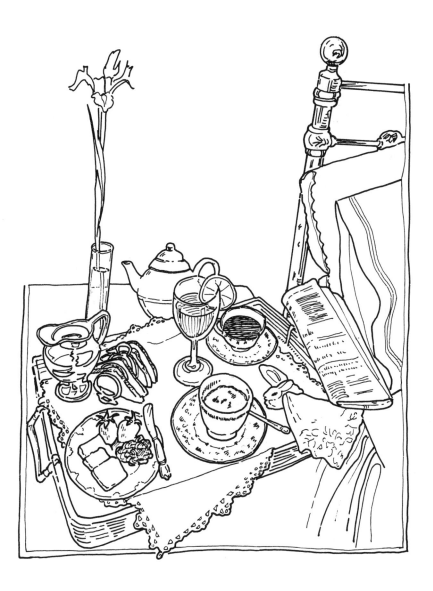

Breakfast Custards
  Basic
  Oatmeal Raisin
  Ginger
  Hot Cocoa
  Maple Syrup
Cheese Oatmeal Custard
Spoon Bread Custard
The Coach House Bread and Butter Pudding
Baked Rice Pudding
  Rose Water Rice Pudding
Indian Pudding
Cornmeal Buttermilk Pudding
Cornflake Pudding
Cottage Cheese Oatmeal Pudding
Sharlotka
Steamed Persimmon Pudding
Dark Steamed Pudding
Maple Oatmeal Steamed Pudding
Sherry and Ginger Steamed Pudding
Steamed Spiced Carrot Pudding

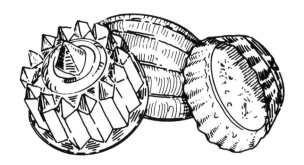

Custards and puddings are wholesome, soft and spoonable, and wonderfully moist—gentle food that won't ruffle your feathers in the morning. A breakfast custard or pudding is a complete breakfast in a bowl, and made from morning ingredients like dairy products, cereals, breads, and eggs. Though they cover a wide range of different flavors, they are essentially simple preparations: if you know how to make one, you can make them all.

Egg custards are quickly made and make great everyday breakfasts. Steamed puddings are sturdier and more cakelike—the perfect breakfast dish for Christmas, Thanksgiving, or Easter.

BREAKFAST CUSTARDS

For people who don't like eggs other ways, soft egg custards slide down deliciously and take no effort to enjoy. They always used to be considered good for the convalescing, and they do seem to be especially digestible and strengthening. Smooth, silky custards are wonderfully receptive to savory additions, and they are easy to make in quantity if you are having a large breakfast party.

Basic Custard

(four servings)

½ cup milk
½ cup heavy cream, or 1 cup
   milk, or 1 cup half-and-half

4 eggs
Salt to taste

Preheat the oven to 375°F. Butter 4 custard cups. Put a shallow baking dish, large enough to hold the custard cups, in the oven and fill it halfway with hot water.

Beat the milk, cream, eggs, and salt together in a bowl. Add the various ingredients for each kind of custard in the manner described in the recipes that follow. Place the filled cups in the water bath in the oven. Bake for 20 minutes, or until the custard is barely set. Remove from the oven. Run a knife around the edges and turn the custards out onto a serving plate; or serve in the cup.

Oatmeal Raisin Custard

½ cup quick oatmeal
3 tablespoons raisins, chopped
½ teaspoon nutmeg

Basic Custard (preceding recipe)
4 teaspoons brown sugar

Stir the oatmeal, chopped raisins, and nutmeg into the custard mixture, and sprinkle the brown sugar on top after filling the custard cups. Serve with bacon.

Ginger Custard

½ cup cream cheese
2 teaspoons grated fresh
  gingerroot

2 tablespoons marmalade
Basic Custard (see page 214)

Stir the cream cheese, ginger, and marmalade into the custard mixture until thoroughly blended before filling the cups. This stays rather creamy in the center, so bake about 25 minutes. Serve with oatmeal and toast.

Hot Cocoa Custard

2 tablespoons unsweetened cocoa
2 tablespoons sugar

¼ cup very hot water
Basic Custard (see page 214)

Mix the cocoa and sugar together in a bowl, add the hot water, and stir to dissolve. Allow to cool a little, then add the ingredients for the basic custard recipe and pour into the custard cups.

Maple Syrup Custard

½ cup maple syrup
Basic Custard (see page 214)

Add the maple syrup to the basic custard recipe and stir to mix. This is one of the best custards I know.

Cheese Oatmeal Custard

(four servings)

This makes a good, wholesome, well-rounded breakfast. A dish of sliced banana and prunes is nice with it.

6 eggs
1½ cups milk (use skim milk
  if you wish)
⅔ cup quick oatmeal

⅔ cup grated Jack cheese
Salt
¾ cup shredded wheat
  (preferably bite-size)

Preheat the oven to 350°F. Butter a 1½-quart casserole.

Stir the eggs and milk together in a bowl. Add the oatmeal, cheese, and salt to taste. Pour into the casserole and strew the shredded wheat on top.

Bake for about 35 to 40 minutes, or until just set. Serve hot.

Spoon Bread Custard

(six servings)

Spoon Bread Custard is moister and lighter than most cornmeal recipes, and it has a little bite to it from the buttermilk. This is very good served with maple syrup.

1 cup yellow cornmeal
2 cups water
1 teaspoon salt

2 tablespoons butter
4 eggs, well beaten
1 cup buttermilk

Preheat the oven to 400°F. Butter a 1½-quart casserole.

Put the cornmeal in a bowl and stir in 1 cup cold water. Put the remaining 1 cup water in a saucepan with the salt and bring to a boil. Immediately stir in the wet cornmeal (wetting cornmeal first with cold water prevents lumping). Stirring constantly, cook for 1 minute. Remove from the heat and beat in the butter, eggs, and buttermilk, beating until smooth. Pour into the casserole and bake about 40 minutes, until a straw inserted into the center comes out clean. Serve hot.

The Coach House
Bread and Butter Pudding

(ten servings)

This is the best bread pudding ever. The recipe comes generously from Leon Lianides, owner of the legendary New York restaurant The Coach House. Don't overbake the pudding—remove it from the oven when the center still trembles slightly.

12 or 13 slices French bread,
    crusts removed (not sourdough)
8 tablespoons (1 stick) butter,
    room temperature
5 eggs
4 egg yolks

1 cup granulated sugar
⅛ teaspoon salt
4 cups milk
1 cup heavy cream
1 tablespoon vanilla extract
Confectioners' sugar for sprinkling

Preheat the oven to 375°F.

Butter one side of each slice of bread and set aside.

Put the eggs, yolks, granulated sugar, and salt in a large bowl and beat until thoroughly mixed.

Pour the milk and cream into a heavy-bottomed saucepan and heat until scalded (tiny bubbles will form around the edge of the pan). Remove from the heat and, whisking briskly, slowly add the egg mixture. Stir in the vanilla.

Have ready enough boiling water to come 2½ inches up the sides of a pot large enough to hold a 2-quart baking dish. Layer the bread, buttered side up, in the baking dish. Strain the custard into the dish (the bread will float to the top). Put the pot of boiling water into the oven and then put the custard-filled dish into it.

Bake about 45 minutes, or until the custard is set except for a slight tremble in the center. Remove from the oven and sprinkle confectioners' sugar on top. It is delicious hot or cold, and just perfect with a little unsweetened heavy cream poured over.

Baked Rice Pudding

(six servings)

This old-fashioned, creamy rice pudding is soft and delicate. It will replace any of your new-fangled rice pudding recipes.

4 cups milk	4 tablespoons rice
½ teaspoon salt	Optional: ½ teaspoon nutmeg
⅔ cup sugar	

Preheat the oven to 300°F.

Put all the ingredients in a buttered baking dish and stir to blend. Bake for 3½ hours, stirring 3 times in the first hour of baking so the rice doesn't settle.

Rose Water Rice Pudding   Follow the above recipe, omitting the nutmeg. Buy rose water (labeled Fluid Rose Soluble) at the pharmacy and dilute half and half with water. Put the mixture in a spray bottle, and just before serving the rice pudding, spray with rose water.

Indian Pudding

(six servings)

This old New England classic bakes basic breakfast ingredients together into a deep, hearty pudding. It is wonderful hot or cold.

4 cups cold milk
½ cup yellow cornmeal
1 cup brown sugar
1½ teaspoons ground ginger
½ teaspoon nutmeg

½ teaspoon cinnamon
1 teaspoon salt
½ cup molasses
1 cup heavy cream

Preheat the oven to 275°F. Butter a 2-quart baking dish.

Stir together 1 cup cold milk and the cornmeal. In a heavy-bottomed saucepan, heat the remaining 3 cups milk to a bare simmer, stir in the cornmeal mixture, and stir briskly until smooth. Stirring constantly, cook about 4 or 5 minutes over medium heat, until the mush is well thickened. Remove from the heat and stir in the sugar, ginger, nutmeg, cinnamon, and salt. Mix well. Add the molasses and cream and blend well.

Pour the mixture into the baking dish and bake for 2 hours. Serve warm with a little heavy cream poured over.

Cornmeal Buttermilk Pudding

(four servings)

This light and spongy pudding is appetizingly tart with buttermilk and lemon zest—it is good with scrambled eggs or sausage.

2 eggs
½ cup yellow cornmeal
2 cups buttermilk

½ teaspoon salt
1 tablespoon grated lemon zest

Preheat the oven to 350°F. Butter a 1½-quart soufflé dish.

Put the eggs in a mixing bowl and whisk until well blended. Stir in the cornmeal, buttermilk, salt, and lemon zest.

Pour the mixture into the buttered dish. Bake for about 45 minutes, or until puffy and set. Serve hot.

Cornflake Pudding

(six servings)

This soft, gentle pudding is slightly crisp on top. It won't startle you first thing in the morning. This pudding can be made ahead and reheated.

4 cups milk
2 eggs
2 tablespoons dark molasses
6 tablespoons sugar

1 teaspoon ground ginger
¾ teaspoon salt
4 cups cornflakes

Preheat the oven to 350°F. Butter a 1½-quart soufflé dish or baking dish. Put a pan large enough to hold the baking dish in the oven and fill it with enough hot water to come halfway up the sides of the baking dish.

Put the milk, eggs, molasses, sugar, ginger, and salt in a bowl and stir briskly until all the ingredients are well mixed. Put the cornflakes in the bottom of the baking dish and pour the milk mixture over. Put the dish into the pan of hot water and bake for 45 to 50 minutes, or until the pudding is set. Serve warm.

Cottage Cheese Oatmeal Pudding

(four servings)

Cottage cheese and oatmeal have a natural affinity, and this recipe combines these two good breakfast ingredients in one dish.

2 cups cottage cheese	6 tablespoons sugar
2 cups cooked oatmeal	½ teaspoon nutmeg
2 eggs	Salt to taste
1 cup milk	

Preheat the oven to 325°F. Butter a 1½-quart baking or soufflé dish.

You can use a food processor or an electric mixer; or mix briskly by hand. Put the cottage cheese, oatmeal, eggs, milk, sugar, nutmeg, and salt in a processor or mixing bowl. Process or mix until the mixture is smooth. Spoon into the buttered dish and bake for about 40 minutes, or until the edges are golden and set. Serve hot or cold, with milk or cream.

Sharlotka

(about eight servings)

Sharlotka is a dark, moist, layered Polish pudding that combines several morning foods—bread, butter, jelly, and fruit: simple and inexpensive ingredients. Serve it with scrambled eggs and ham, bacon, or sausage.

A 1-pound loaf dark rye or
   pumpernickel bread
8 tablespoons (1 stick) butter
½ cup sugar
½ cup red wine or apple cider
2 tablespoons lemon juice
1 tablespoon grated lemon zest

1 tablespoon grated orange zest
2 teaspoons cinnamon
2 teaspoons vanilla extract
½ teaspoon salt
10 tart apples (about 4 pounds)
1 cup currant or raspberry jelly,
   melted

Tear the bread into ½-inch pieces. Melt the butter in a large skillet, and when it is sizzling, toss in the bread. Fry the bread lightly for about 7 to 10 minutes over moderately high heat, stirring the bread and shaking the pan frequently to prevent scorching. Remove the pan from the heat and add the sugar, wine or cider, lemon juice, lemon zest, orange zest, cinnamon, vanilla, and salt. Stir until completely blended. Set aside while you prepare the apples.

Preheat the oven to 350°F. Butter a 2-quart baking dish.

Peel the apples, halve them, and remove the cores. Cut each half into 4 wedges. Steam the apple wedges on a rack over boiling water in a covered pan for 10 to 15 minutes, just until the apples are tender when pierced—don't overcook and let them become mushy.

Sprinkle about 1 cup bread mixture in the buttered baking dish. Spread an even layer of cooked apples over the top. Then spread on a generous cup bread mixture and top with the remaining apples. Drizzle the jelly over all, then top with the last of the bread mixture, which will not make a solid layer, but will have a dappled appearance.

Bake for 1 hour, until the top crumbs are crisp and the juices are bubbling. Serve warm, with milk poured over each serving if you wish.

Steamed Persimmon Pudding

(eight servings)

There are persimmon puddings and there are persimmon puddings. This ends the search—it is the best. The color is dark, the texture moist, and the flavor full and spicy. The pudding can be made ahead and reheated; it can even be frozen.

1 cup puréed persimmons (about 3 persimmons with skins removed)	1 tablespoon lemon juice
	2 tablespoons rum
2 teaspoons baking soda	1 cup all-purpose flour
8 tablespoons (1 stick) butter, room temperature	1 teaspoon cinnamon
	½ teaspoon salt
1½ cups sugar	1 cup broken walnuts or pecans
2 eggs	1 cup raisins

Fill a kettle that is large enough to hold a 2-quart pudding mold with enough water to come halfway up the sides of the mold. Let the water come to a boil over medium heat while you are mixing the pudding batter. The mold must have a lid or be snugly covered with foil while steaming (a coffee can with a plastic lid works well). Also there must be a rack or Mason jar ring on the bottom under the mold in the kettle to allow the water to circulate freely while the pudding is steaming. Grease the mold.

Put the persimmon purée in a small bowl and stir in the baking soda. Set aside while mixing the other ingredients (the persimmon mixture will become quite stiff).

Cream the butter and sugar. Add the eggs, lemon juice, and rum, and beat well. Add the flour, cinnamon, and salt, and stir to blend. Add the persimmon mixture. Beat until well mixed. Stir in the nuts and raisins.

Spoon the batter into the mold, cover, and steam for 2 hours. Remove from the kettle, and let rest for 5 minutes. Turn onto a rack to cool, or cool just a little and serve warm. Serve with unsweetened whipped cream.

Dark Steamed Pudding

(eight servings)

This is a good old New England recipe. I love this kind of list of ingredients — all ever-ready straight off the pantry shelf. Together the coffee, spices, and molasses give this pudding a deep rich taste.

2 cups all-purpose flour
1/2 teaspoon ground cloves
1 teaspoon cinnamon
1 teaspoon nutmeg
1/2 teaspoon baking soda
1/2 teaspoon salt
8 tablespoons (1 stick) butter,
   room temperature

1/2 cup dark molasses
1/2 cup coffee
1 cup brown sugar
2 eggs, room temperature
1 1/2 cups broken walnuts

Put a kettle or Dutch oven on the stove and fill one-third full of water. Bring to a simmer. Grease a 2 1/2-quart pudding mold.

Put the flour, cloves, cinnamon, nutmeg, baking soda, and salt in a mixing bowl and stir to blend.

Put the butter, molasses, coffee, brown sugar, and eggs in a large mixing bowl. Beat until smooth. Add the flour mixture and blend well. Stir in the walnuts. Spoon the batter into the mold. Cover snugly. Place a rack or Mason jar ring under the mold on the bottom of the kettle so the pudding mold sits a little above the bottom of the kettle—the water must circulate on the bottom. Cover the kettle. Keep the water about halfway up the side of the mold. The water should be simmering. Steam for 1½ hours. Check the pudding for doneness by inserting a wooden skewer into the center—it is done when it comes out clean. Remove from the kettle and let rest for 10 minutes, uncovered. Invert onto a rack and cool a little. This is to be served warm; it can be made ahead and reheated.

Maple Oatmeal Steamed Pudding

(four servings)

This is a nice change from the traditional steamed pudding: it doesn't have to steam for two hours, it only has four ingredients, and the maple-flavored oats give the pudding a unique, moist texture.

4 cups rolled oats	½ cup maple syrup
3 cups milk	1 teaspoon salt

Butter a 1½-quart soufflé dish or mold. Fill a kettle or Dutch oven with water that will come halfway up the sides of the pudding container. Bring to a boil.

Put the oats, milk, maple syrup, and salt in the dish or mold and stir to mix well. Cover with a lid or a piece of foil, pinching the edges to seal.

Put the mold in the kettle on a rack or Mason jar ring so the mold is off the bottom of the kettle (the water must circulate freely). Put a lid on the kettle and turn the heat down so that the water simmers. Steam for 1 hour. For a firmer pudding, steam for 2 hours. Remove from the kettle, spoon from the mold, and serve hot.

Sherry and Ginger Steamed Pudding

(eight servings)

This pudding has a fine texture and lots of lively flavor. It is one of the best steamed puddings I know of and would be very appropriate for a late Thanksgiving or Christmas breakfast. To make it very special, serve with softly mounded whipped cream that has a little sherry added to it.

10 tablespoons (1 stick plus
   2 tablespoons) butter
1 cup sugar
2 eggs
1½ cups all-purpose flour
1½ teaspoons baking powder
½ teaspoon salt

½ cup sweet or dry sherry
   (do not use cooking sherry)
¾ cup coarsely chopped
   preserved ginger
½ cup ginger marmalade
   (use orange marmalade if
   ginger is not available)

Butter a 2-quart covered pudding mold. Bring a pot of water to a boil—have enough water in the pot so the pudding mold will have water halfway up its sides while steaming.

Beat the butter and sugar in a medium-size bowl until smooth and blended. Add the eggs and beat well. Put the flour, baking powder, and salt in another bowl and stir with a fork until well mixed. Add the dry ingredients to the butter mixture and mix well again. Stir in the sherry and chopped ginger to blend thoroughly.

Spread the marmalade over the bottom of the mold and spoon in the batter. Cover. Put a trivet or Mason jar ring in the pot of water and place the pudding mold on it—the mold must have water circulating around the bottom. Cover the pot and steam for about 1 hour. The water should be kept at a gentle boil. During the steaming check the pot once or twice and replenish with boiling water when necessary.

The pudding is done when a straw inserted into the center comes out clean.

Remove the mold from the water. Allow the pudding to rest for 5 minutes in the mold before turning out onto a rack to cool. Wrap and freeze if the pudding is to be eaten later. To reheat, wrap the pudding in foil and place in a 350°F oven for 30 minutes.

Steamed Spiced Carrot Pudding
(eight servings)

This fine steamed pudding gracefully combines spices and molasses with the natural sweetness of carrots. Serve warm slices with Breakfast Cheese (see page 286) and sliced cantaloupe.

1/2 cup shortening	1 teaspoon cinnamon
1/2 cup sugar	1 teaspoon ground ginger
2 eggs	1/2 teaspoon ground cloves
1 cup dark molasses	1/2 teaspoon nutmeg
1 cup hot water	1/2 teaspoon allspice
2 1/2 cups all-purpose flour	1 1/2 cups grated carrots
1 1/2 teaspoons baking soda	1 cup raisins
1/2 teaspoon salt	

Fill a kettle that is large enough to hold a 2-quart mold with enough water to come halfway up the sides of the mold. Put the kettle over medium heat and let the water come to a boil while you are preparing the pudding batter. The mold must have a lid or be snugly covered with foil while steaming (a coffee can with a plastic lid will work). Put a rack or a Mason jar ring on the bottom of the kettle so that water can circulate under the mold while steaming. Grease the mold.

Put the shortening and sugar in a mixing bowl and beat until smooth. Add the eggs and mix well. Add the molasses and hot water and beat briskly. Stir in the flour, baking soda, salt, cinnamon, ginger, cloves, nutmeg, and allspice. Beat until well blended. Stir in the carrots and raisins.

Spoon the batter into the mold, cover, and let steam for 2½ hours. Remove the mold from the kettle and let sit for 5 minutes. Turn onto a rack and let cool a little. Serve warm.

Cookies, Pies, and Cakes

Mother's Cookies
English Digestives
Cereal Cookies
Oatmeal Bran Breakfast Cookies
Orange Marmalade Cookies
Ginger Shortbread
Gingersnaps
Hard Ginger Cakes

Basic Pie Dough
Breakfast Apple Pie
Hominy Grits Pie
Apricot Shortbread Pie
Cranberry Raisin Pie
Shaker Stacked Pie
Mother's Pie
   Milk Pie

Whole Wheat Sponge Roll
Lemon Pound Cake
Granola Pound Cake
Raisin Almond Breakfast Cake
Indian Loaf Cake
Madeira Poppy Seed Cake
Fresh Ginger Cake
Soft Gingerbread
Great Coffee Cake
   Raisin and Spice
   Dried Fig and Almond
   Apple and Walnut
   Simple Vanilla
Fluffy Caramel Coffee Cake
Almond Coconut Coffee Cake
Apricot Prune Coffee Cake

These cookies, pies, and cakes are just good breakfast ingredients in another form, and they can make complete breakfasts along with fresh fruit or fruit juice, although we get so stuck in habit and tradition that we might not recognize these things right away as typical breakfast foods.

The cookie recipes are not too sweet. Cookies are made ahead as a matter of course, so they're on hand for an instant portable breakfast when you want to walk around in the morning and survey the day ahead. Cookies are perfect to take along with a thermos of coffee to the fireplace in cold weather, or out to the patio when it is warm out.

I guess that one reason we eat pie for breakfast is because it's there from last night's supper. I can think of nothing more appealing than several warm, plump pies laid out for the morning meal—there is something old-fashioned and homey about it. If you have a hard time arousing breakfast appetites, pies are a sure-fire way to get everyone to clean their plates.

The breakfast cakes in this chapter are meant to be sliced, toasted, and buttered, not frosted. With good cake the wholesomeness will shine through without the added frill of frosting. Breakfast cakes are wonderful, particularly if you are a sweet and not a savory breakfast person.

Mother's Cookies

(three dozen cookies)

I like to think that this is the cookie that all mothers would make if they knew about it. These cookies are crisp, and filled with irregular crunch and raisins.

½ cup shortening	1 teaspoon cinnamon
¾ cup sugar	¾ cup all-purpose flour
1 egg	½ cup rolled oats
½ teaspoon baking soda	1 cup cornflakes or Wheaties
½ teaspoon salt	¾ cup golden raisins

Preheat the oven to 350°F. Don't grease the baking sheet(s).

Put the shortening, sugar, and egg in a mixing bowl. Beat until smooth. Add the baking soda, salt, cinnamon, and flour and beat until well blended. Add the oats, cornflakes or Wheaties, and raisins. This is going to be a stiff dough, but exert a little vigor and stir until the oats, flakes, and raisins are well distributed.

Drop rounded tablespoons of dough onto the baking sheet(s) about 1 inch apart. Bake for 15 to 17 minutes, or until lightly golden. Remove from the oven and let cool.

English Digestives

(six dozen biscuits)

These biscuits grow on you; in spite of yourself you will be reaching for one more. Wheat flour with bits of bran mixed in makes the best biscuit. These are mildly sweet and go well with a dish of fruit and coffee or tea.

1 cup all-purpose flour	8 tablespoons (1 stick) butter,
1½ cups whole wheat flour	chilled
¼ cup bran	¾ cup brown sugar
½ teaspoon baking powder	1 egg, well beaten
¼ teaspoon baking soda	½ cup water
½ teaspoon salt	

Preheat the oven to 375°F. Grease the baking sheets.

Put the flours, bran, baking powder, baking soda, and salt in a mixing bowl. Stir with a fork to mix well.

Cut the butter into small pieces and add to the flour mixture. Using either a pastry blender or your fingers, cut or rub the butter into the flour mixture until it is in coarse small bits. Add the sugar and, using a fork or your fingers, toss the mixture until the sugar is well distributed. Stir in the egg and water. Mix until you can gather the dough in a rough ball, and place on a floured surface. Knead about a dozen times. Divide into three equal pieces. Roll one piece out about ⅛ inch thick. Cut into 2½-inch rounds and place on a greased baking sheet. Prick each biscuit two or three times on top with the tines of a fork. Repeat with the other two pieces.

Bake about 20 minutes, or until the biscuits are lightly browned around the edges and on the bottom. Remove and cool. Store in an airtight container, or freeze.

Cereal Cookies

(thirty-two cookies)

These cookies are crisp and good, particularly with warm rice pudding. You may use either oatmeal or granola in the dough.

8 tablespoons (1 stick) butter, softened
⅓ cup brown sugar
⅔ cup granulated sugar
1 teaspoon vanilla extract
1 egg
1½ cups all-purpose flour

½ teaspoon baking soda
½ teaspoon salt
1 cup rolled oats or unsweetened granola (see page 91 for homemade)
1 cup broken walnuts

Preheat the oven to 350°F. Grease two baking sheets.

Cream the butter and sugars until smooth. Add the vanilla and egg and beat well. Stir in the flour, baking soda, and salt. Mix vigorously. Add the cereal and walnuts. Blend well.

Lightly flour a board and turn the dough onto it. Roll out the dough about ⅛ inch thick. Cut the cookies out with a 3-inch cookie cutter. Place the cookies slightly apart (they don't spread) on the baking sheets.

Bake for about 12 minutes, or until the cookies are lightly browned. Remove from the oven and cool on racks or on pieces of waxed paper.

Oatmeal Bran Breakfast Cookies

(three dozen cookies)

These chewy, crunchy cookies need no introduction.

¾ cup vegetable shortening
1 cup brown sugar
⅓ cup granulated sugar
¼ cup strong coffee
1 egg

2½ cups rolled oats
1 cup all-purpose flour
1 teaspoon salt
½ teaspoon baking soda
1½ cups All-Bran cereal

Preheat the oven to 350°F. Don't grease the baking sheet(s).

Put the shortening, sugars, coffee, and egg in a mixing bowl and beat until smooth and blended. Add the oats, flour, salt, and baking soda. Stir very well so the dough is well mixed.

Spread the All-Bran cereal out on a piece of waxed paper. This is a sticky dough, so wet your fingers with cold water before pinching off about 2 tablespoons of dough at a time and rolling it in the All-Bran. Don't worry if you can't get a heavy coating of cereal on each piece of dough; if just a little of the All-Bran sticks, it will give a nice texture to the cookies.

Place the dough pieces about 1½ inches apart on the baking sheet(s). Bake 12 to 15 minutes. Remove from the oven and cool on racks.

Orange Marmalade Cookies

(three dozen cookies)

This is an old-fashioned cookie that is rather thick and chewy with plenty of tasty orange marmalade in it. Orange Marmalade Cookies make splendid dunkers with coffee.

2 eggs
1½ cups sugar
1 teaspoon salt
⅓ cup shortening, melted and
  cooled
¾ cup orange marmalade

Grated zest of 1 lemon
3 tablespoons freshly squeezed
  lemon juice
3 cups all-purpose flour
2 teaspoons baking powder
1 cup broken walnuts

Preheat the oven to 375°F. Grease the baking sheet(s).

Put the eggs and sugar in a mixing bowl and beat until blended. Add the salt, shortening, orange marmalade, lemon zest, and lemon juice. Beat until the dough is thoroughly mixed. Add the flour and baking powder and beat well. This is a stiff dough. Add the walnuts, stirring well to distribute.

Drop the cookies by tablespoons onto the baking sheet(s) about 1 inch apart. Bake about 12 minutes, or until the edges of the cookies are golden. Remove from the oven and cool.

Ginger Shortbread

(two dozen wedges)

A crunchy, buttery cookie with a smooth texture and spicy overtones of ginger. The dough is pressed into pans like a plain shortbread, then cut into wedges while still warm and soft; it will crisp as it cools. Serve with fresh or poached fruit, or at the end of breakfast with coffee.

2 cups all-purpose flour	1 teaspoon baking soda
1 cup dark brown sugar	½ pound (2 sticks) butter,
2 tablespoons ground ginger	softened

Preheat the oven to 325°F, and get out two 8-inch round cake pans.

In a large bowl, stir and toss together the flour, brown sugar, ginger, and baking soda until thoroughly mixed. Cut the butter into half-tablespoon bits and drop them in. Blend the butter into the dry ingredients, using your fingertips or a pastry blender, as you would mix a pie dough, until the mixture is crumbly and you see no unblended pieces of butter.

Divide the dough in half and press each piece evenly into each of the cake pans. Prick all over with a fork at half-inch intervals. Bake for 40 to 45 minutes, until lightly browned around the edges—the center will stay low, and only the sides will rise slightly. Remove from the oven and let cool a minute or two, then cut each pan into 12 pie-shaped wedges. Lift from the pans and let cool completely on racks. Store in airtight containers.

Gingersnaps

(about forty cookies)

You will find these to be the best-tasting spicy, crisp gingersnaps there
are. They are sweeter than most of the other breakfast cookies. Serve
them at breakfast with sliced bananas and cream and you could start a
trend. Try crumbling the gingersnaps over oatmeal or any other cooked
cereal.

¾ cup vegetable shortening
1 cup sugar, plus extra to roll
    the cookies in
1 egg
¼ cup molasses

2 cups all-purpose flour
2 teaspoons baking soda
½ teaspoon salt
1 tablespoon ground ginger
1 teaspoon cinnamon

Preheat the oven to 350°F and grease some cookie sheets.

Beat together the shortening and 1 cup sugar. Add the egg, beat
until light and fluffy, and then add the molasses. In a separate bowl,
stir and toss together the flour, baking soda, salt, ginger, and cinnamon.
Add the dry ingredients to the first mixture, and beat until smooth
and blended.

Gather up bits of the dough and roll them between the palms of
your hands into 1-inch balls, then roll each ball in sugar. Place about 2
inches apart on the prepared cookie sheets and bake for 10 to 12
minutes, until the cookies have spread and the tops have cracked.
Remove from the oven, take the gingersnaps off the baking sheet, and
let cool on a rack.

Hard Ginger Cakes

(about forty-eight bars)

In the nineteenth century, hard ginger cakes were called ginger cookies and soft ginger cakes were known as gingerbread. This recipe makes a highly spiced ginger cookie.

2 cups all-purpose flour
1 cup firmly packed brown sugar
1 tablespoon ground ginger
1 teaspoon baking soda

½ teaspoon salt
8 tablespoons (1 stick) butter,
   room temperature

Preheat the oven to 325°F. Use an ungreased 7- or 8-inch square pan.

Put the flour, brown sugar, ginger, baking soda, and salt in a mixing bowl, and stir until well mixed. Add the butter and mix with a fork until well blended.

Press the mixture into the pan—it should be about ½ inch thick or a little thinner. Bake for 45 minutes to 1 hour. Remove and cut the cookies into finger-size bars, about ½ inch by 2 inches. Let cool in the pan. Remove from the pan, break up into bars, and store in an airtight container.

Basic Pie Dough

(for a 9-inch two-crust pie)

2¼ cups all-purpose flour   ¾ cup vegetable shortening
½ teaspoon salt   6 to 7 tablespoons cold water

Put the flour and salt in a mixing bowl and stir to blend, using a fork. Add the shortening, and, using your fingertips, a pastry blender, or two dinner knives, mix the fat and flour together (don't blend—the fat must remain in small pieces) until the mixture resembles coarse bread crumbs.

Add the water, a tablespoon or two at a time, gently stirring with a fork to distribute evenly. Add only enough water to allow the dough to be picked up and held together in a rough mass.

Sprinkle a board amply with flour and divide the dough into two pieces, one a little larger than the other. Roll the smaller piece out on the board into a circle 2 inches larger than the pie plate. Roll the dough up on the rolling pin and, starting on the far side of the pie plate, unroll the dough so that it is draped into the plate. Do not stretch the dough.

Add the filling, spreading it evenly. Roll the second piece of dough into a circle about 2½ inches larger than the pie plate. Again roll it upon the rolling pin and unroll over the filled shell, beginning from the far side of the pie plate. Turn the edges of the dough under and crimp neatly. Cut 2 or 3 heat vents on the top before baking.

Breakfast Apple Pie

(six servings)

A warm piece of apple pie, a small piece of Cheddar cheese, and a cup of hot coffee make a splendid breakfast. If they served this pie at truck stops, I'd become a truck driver.

1 cup cornflakes
One unbaked 8- or 9-inch pie
  shell (preceding recipe)
5 large, tart apples, peeled, cored,
  and cut into tenths
½ cup sugar
1 teaspoon cinnamon

Topping
¾ cup all-purpose flour
½ cup sugar
7 tablespoons butter, chilled and
  cut into small pieces

Preheat the oven to 450°F.

Sprinkle the cornflakes evenly over the pie shell. Toss the apple slices, sugar, and cinnamon together in a large mixing bowl until all the apple slices are coated. Spread the apple mixture over the pie shell.

Make the topping. Put the flour, sugar, and butter in a bowl. Using a pastry blender or your fingers, work the butter into the flour until the mixture resembles irregular bread crumbs. Sprinkle the crumbs evenly over the apple slices.

Bake the pie for 10 minutes at 450°F, then reduce the heat to 350°F and continue to bake for about 35 minutes, or until the apples are tender and bubbling. Serve warm with a piece of Cheddar cheese on the side.

Hominy Grits Pie

(six servings)

Grits, believe it or not, make a creamy, delicate pie. I tried adding ½ cup raspberries to the filling and the flavor was fabulous.

3 eggs
1 cup cooked grits
½ cup light brown sugar
⅓ cup heavy cream

One unbaked 8- or 9-inch pie shell (see page 240)
Optional: ½ cup fresh berries or sliced fruit

Preheat the oven to 400°F.

Put the eggs in a mixing bowl and beat until blended and smooth. Stir in the grits, sugar, and cream and mix until blended. Pour the mixture into the pie shell, and gently stir in the berries or fruit, if you are using them.

Bake for about 40 minutes, or until the center is a trifle jiggly but most of the filling is set. Cool for 5 minutes after removing from the oven. Serve warm or cold.

Apricot Shortbread Pie

(eight servings)

The shortbread crust in this pie is crisp and butter-golden, and the apricot filling is tart, sweet, and boldly fresh. Apricot Shortbread Pie with a glass of milk makes a nice small breakfast.

8 tablespoons (1 stick) butter, room temperature
1⅓ cups all-purpose flour
1 cup granulated sugar, approximately
1½ cups pitted and coarsely chopped fresh apricots

¼ cup water
1 egg, well beaten
¼ teaspoon salt
½ teaspoon baking powder
Confectioners' sugar

Preheat the oven to 375°F.

Put the butter, 1 cup flour, and ⅓ cup sugar in a mixing bowl and, using your hands or a large spoon, blend until the mixture is smooth. Pat the dough evenly over the bottom of a 9-inch pie pan. Bake about 25 minutes, or until the crust is lightly golden.

While the crust is baking, put the apricots and water into a skillet and turn the heat to high. When the fruit begins to bubble, turn the heat down to medium, stirring often so the fruit doesn't scorch. Cook until the fruit is thickened. Remove from the heat and let cool a little. Stir the egg into the apricots and blend well. Add up to ¾ cup sugar (depending on how sweet the apricots are), the remaining ⅓ cup flour, the salt, and the baking powder. Beat until all the lumps are gone.

Spread the apricot mixture over the pie crust and bake about 25 minutes, or until the topping is puffy. Remove and shake confectioners' sugar over the top. Cut into 8 wedges and serve.

Cranberry Raisin Pie

(six to eight servings)

Cranberry Raisin Pie is a delicious combination of tart and sweet with a touch of orange, and is especially good when eaten warm. It is just the ticket for Christmas morning served with eggnog.

2 cups raisins	¼ cup Grand Marnier
4 cups fresh cranberries	2 teaspoons grated orange zest
2 tablespoons all-purpose flour	Basic Pie Dough for a 2-crust pie
1 cup sugar	(see page 240)

Put the raisins in a bowl, add water to cover, and soak for at least 2 hours. Drain. Preheat the oven to 400°F.

Put the raisins and cranberries in a mixing bowl. In a small bowl, stir the flour into the sugar, mixing well, and sprinkle over the raisin-cranberry mixture. Add the Grand Marnier and orange zest. Toss all together until the fruit is thoroughly coated.

Line an 8- or 9-inch pie plate with pie dough and spread the filling evenly over. Cover the filling with pie dough, seal, and flute the edges.

Bake the pie for 15 minutes at 400°F, then reduce the heat to 350°F and bake for 45 minutes more, or until the juices bubble. Cool a bit before serving.

Shaker Stacked Pie

(twelve servings)

The Shakers have made a great contribution to American cooking with the simplicity, freshness, and good taste of their food. Stacked pie was born of the need for Shaker women to carry many pies to church suppers easily. Instead of trying to handle three or more separate pies, their clever solution was a many-layered pie. This version is not as deep and thick as the original, but it gives you the idea, and it is delicious for breakfast.

Pie Pastry
3 cups all-purpose flour
1 teaspoon salt
1 cup vegetable shortening
3/4 cup water, approximately

Filling
2 cups milk
1/2 cup sugar
6 tablespoons all-purpose flour
1/2 teaspoon salt
8 egg yolks, slightly beaten
4 teaspoons vanilla extract
4 tablespoons (1/2 stick) butter

Preheat the oven to 425°F.

Mix together the flour and salt in a bowl. Add the shortening and, using your fingers or a pastry blender, mix the mass until it looks like irregular bread crumbs. While stirring with a fork, slowly add the water. You may need more or less water, but use enough to bring the dough together into a rough ball. Divide the dough into 4 balls — one should be about one-third larger than the others.

Dust a board with flour and roll the biggest ball into a circle large enough to line a 9- or 10-inch pie pan. Put the rolled pastry into the pie pan and flute the edges. Prick the bottom and sides all over with a fork, then line the pie pan with a heavy piece of foil to hold the pastry down. Bake for about 6 minutes, remove the foil, and bake for 5 minutes more.

Roll the other 3 balls into rounds the diameter of the pie pan (roll them thin). Place the 3 rounds on baking sheets and bake from 8 to 10 minutes, or until they are lightly colored. Remove the 3 pastries from the oven and gently place them on waxed paper to cool (don't worry if they break; you can put them back together when you are assembling the pie).

To make the filling, heat the milk until just before boiling (tiny bubbles will form around the edge of the pan). Meanwhile, stir together the sugar, flour, and salt in a mixing bowl until blended. Slowly add the hot milk, a little at a time, to the flour mixture, whisking or stirring briskly all the while. Return the milk-flour mixture back to the saucepan and cook, stirring, until it boils and becomes smooth and thick.

Put the slightly beaten egg yolks into a bowl; slowly spoon a few tablespoons of the thickened sauce into the yolks and blend. Pour the yolks into the sauce and cook, stirring constantly for another minute or so—allow the sauce to boil while you are doing this. Remove from the heat and put the filling into a bowl. Stir in the vanilla and butter. Either spread a film of butter over the top of the filling or cover with waxed paper so a crust won't form. Cool, then chill, until you are ready to assemble and serve the pie.

The pie is assembled with alternate layers of pastry and filling. First spread one quarter of the filling into the pastry shell, place the first round of pastry on top, and spread over it another quarter of the filling. Stack the second round of pastry on top, spread over that another layer of filling, place the third disk of pastry on top, and finish with the rest of the filling.

Mother's Pie

(six servings)

Mother's Pie and Milk Pie are surprisingly good, even though they are just ways to use leftover scraps of pie dough. Children have loved this for ages, and it would be a special treat to serve it for breakfast the day after a good report card.

Enough pie dough for an 8- or 9-inch pie shell*	3 tablespoons sugar
3 tablespoons flour	½ teaspoon cinnamon
	1 cup milk

*NOTE: If you have only a little leftover pie dough, roll out whatever scraps you have to about ⅛ inch thick, crimp the edge, and reduce the other ingredients proportionately.

Preheat the oven to 400°F.

Roll out the pie dough scraps into one piece and place it in a pie tin. Stir the flour, sugar, and cinnamon together in a small bowl. Sprinkle over the pie dough. Pour the milk over and bake for about 35 minutes. Even if the milk still seems liquid, remove and let cool for 10 minutes—it will set and be perfect. Slice and eat warm.

Milk Pie   Proceed as above but use a mixture of ¼ cup sugar and ½ teaspoon cinnamon and sprinkle it evenly over the pie dough. Pour ⅓ cup milk on top and smooth over with your fingers or a spoon. Bake for 30 minutes, or until the crust is golden. Cool for 10 minutes. Serve warm.

Whole Wheat Sponge Roll

(about ten servings)

This simplest of recipes makes the lightest, best sponge roll I know. Fill it with Date Raisin Condiment (see page 277), or Lemon Curd (see page 274), or spread thinly with whipped cottage cheese and cover with soft sliced fresh fruit or berries. Roll this sponge wide side up so you can have a long roll that will provide about ten good portions. This roll can be baked the night before serving, rolled up in a tea towel, and left at room temperature until morning to fill and serve. If you wish to make this into a dessert roll, use all cake flour.

5 eggs	1/2 teaspoon baking powder
1/2 cup granulated sugar	1/4 teaspoon salt
1/4 cup whole wheat flour	1 teaspoon vanilla extract
1/4 cup cake flour	Confectioners' sugar for sprinkling

Preheat the oven to 350°F. Grease a 15½- × 10½- × 1-inch jelly-roll pan and line with waxed paper. Grease and lightly flour the waxed paper.

Put the eggs and sugar into a mixing bowl and beat for about 4 minutes (an electric mixer is almost a must for this recipe), until pale, fluffy, and light.

Mix the flours, baking powder, and salt in a bowl, stirring with a fork to blend well. Turn the mixer to the lowest speed and sprinkle the flour mixture and the vanilla over the egg mixture, mixing for just a few seconds. Remove the bowl from the mixer and, using a spatula, gently finish folding the flour into the egg mixture until no white streaks show.

Spread the batter evenly in the jelly-roll pan. Bake for about 12 minutes, or until the top of the cake is golden.

Spread a tea towel on the counter and sift a little confectioners' sugar evenly over the towel. Invert the cake onto the towel. Remove the waxed paper and roll the cake wide side up in the towel. Leave rolled up until you are ready to fill it. Unroll, spread the filling evenly over the roll, reroll, place on a serving plate, and sprinkle the top with confectioners' sugar. Slice and serve.

Lemon Pound Cake

(one large loaf)

The use of cake flour in this recipe gives this pound cake an extra-fine crumb and a delicate texture that suits its lemon flavor. But all-purpose flour will work well, too.

½ pound (2 sticks) butter, room temperature	2 cups cake flour
1⅔ cups sugar	½ teaspoon salt
5 eggs, room temperature	2 teaspoons grated lemon zest (the yellow outer rind of the lemon)

Preheat the oven to 325°F. Grease and flour a 9 × 5 × 3-inch loaf pan.

Put the butter in a large mixing bowl and beat until creamy. Slowly add the sugar, beating constantly, until the mixture is well blended. Add the eggs, one at a time, beating well after each addition. Add the flour and salt and beat until smooth and thoroughly blended. Add the lemon zest and beat another few seconds.

Pour the batter into the pan and smooth the top with a spatula. Bake for about an hour, or until a straw comes out clean when inserted into the center. Let cool in the pan 5 minutes before turning onto a rack to cool completely.

Granola Pound Cake

(one medium loaf)

This cake has only half the usual amount of sugar and, though mildly sweet, it is the combination of delicate crumb and good granola crunch that makes it special. Sliced, toasted, and buttered, it is wonderful.

½ pound (2 sticks) butter,
   room temperature
1 cup sugar
2 teaspoons vanilla extract
5 eggs, room temperature

1 cup all-purpose flour
1 cup cake flour
½ teaspoon salt
1¼ cups granola (see page 90
   for homemade granola)

Preheat the oven to 325°F. Butter an 8 × 5 × 3-inch loaf pan.

Combine the butter and sugar in a mixing bowl and beat until smooth. Add the vanilla and the eggs, one at a time, beating until very well mixed. Add the flours and salt and beat at least 2 minutes. Stir in the granola.

Spoon the batter into the loaf pan and bake for 45 to 55 minutes, or until a straw comes out clean when inserted into the center. Gently remove the cake from the pan and let cool on a rack.

Raisin Almond Breakfast Cake

(one round cake)

A complete breakfast in just one dish, this cake is made from milk, cream, eggs, wheat, raisins, and almonds. Serve warm with whipped cream, or with some heavy cream poured on top.

1 cup milk and 1 cup cream (or 2 cups milk)	2 eggs, lightly beaten
1/3 cup plus 2 tablespoons sugar	1/4 teaspoon almond extract
1/2 teaspoon salt	1 cup chopped almonds
3/4 cup Cream of Wheat (or Cream of Rice or Quick Grits)	1 cup golden raisins
	1/3 cup whole wheat bread crumbs

Preheat the oven to 350°F. Butter a baking dish, 7 inches in diameter and about 2 inches deep.

Put the milk, cream, 1/3 cup sugar, and the salt in a heavy-bottomed saucepan. Bring to a boil and slowly stir in the Cream of Wheat. Stir constantly over medium heat until the mixture has thickened. Remove from the heat and blend a little of the hot milk mixture into the eggs, stirring constantly. Add the eggs to the milk mixture and beat until well blended. Stir in the almond extract, almonds, and raisins.

Mix the whole wheat bread crumbs with the remaining 2 tablespoons sugar in a small bowl. Sprinkle the crumbs generously over the bottom and sides of the buttered baking dish. Spoon in the mixture. Bake for 30 minutes. Remove and let rest for 5 minutes. Invert the cake onto a serving plate and serve hot in wedges with cream.

Indian Loaf Cake

(one medium loaf cake)

If you are a cornmeal fan you'll like this recipe for a mildly sweet cake with walnuts and raisins. Serve warm slices of this with applesauce.

1 cup yellow cornmeal
2 cups cold water
½ cup brown sugar
½ teaspoon salt

5 tablespoons butter
1 cup coarsely chopped walnuts
1 cup golden raisins

Butter an 8½ × 4½ × 3-inch loaf pan. Put the cornmeal in a bowl with 1 cup water, stir, and let stand while you put together the rest of the ingredients.

Put the remaining 1 cup water in a pan and add the brown sugar, salt, and butter. Turn the heat to medium and, stirring constantly, bring the sugar mixture to a boil. Cook for 1 minute. Stir in the cornmeal mixture. Stirring briskly and constantly, cook for about 5 minutes, or until the mixture is very stiff and comes away from the sides of the pan. Remove from the heat and add the walnuts and raisins.

Spread the stiff cornmeal into the loaf pan. Let cool, cover with plastic wrap, and refrigerate until needed. When ready to serve, slice and warm the slices before serving.

Madeira Poppy Seed Cake

(one 10-inch tube cake)

This cake is lighter than light, and quite perfect for that small second breakfast late in the morning. It can also be made into two 9- by 5- by 3-inch loaves with a little batter left over for a few cupcakes. Freezing is kind to this cake.

2⅓ cups cake flour	5 egg yolks
1⅓ cups sugar	¾ cup Madeira wine
1 tablespoon baking powder	1 cup egg whites (6 or 7 whites)
1 teaspoon salt	½ teaspoon cream of tartar
½ cup vegetable oil	½ cup (2-ounce can) poppy seeds

Preheat the oven to 325°F. Don't grease the tube pan, but if you are using loaf pans and muffin tins, grease and lightly flour them.

Sift the flour, 1 cup sugar, baking powder, and salt together into a mixing bowl. Add the oil, yolks, and Madeira. Beat briskly until smooth.

Put the egg whites in an electric mixer bowl. Beat for a few seconds until the whites are frothy. Add the cream of tartar and continue to beat on high speed until the whites form soft peaks. Still beating on high speed, slowly add the remaining ⅓ cup sugar. Beat until very stiff. Turn the mixer to the lowest speed and add the yolk mixture and the poppy seeds. Beat for just a few seconds until the batter looks blended. Remove from the mixer and use the spatula for a few folds to blend the batter completely.

Pour into the pan(s) and bake. A tube cake takes about 1 hour, loaves about 45 minutes, and cupcakes about 20 minutes. They are done when a straw inserted into the center comes out clean. Let the tube cake cool completely in its pan, turned upside down. Cool the loaves and cupcakes for 10 minutes in their pans, and remove to cool on racks.

Fresh Ginger Cake

(two 8-inch cakes)

This is a lovely, delicate cake. Frost with faintly sweetened whipped cream that has finely chopped crystallized ginger added. Slices of fresh mango around the bottom of the cake would be perfection.

¼ cup fresh gingerroot, unpeeled, cut into large chunks
1 cup sugar
3 tablespoons lemon zest with a little white pith
8 tablespoons (1 stick) unsalted butter, room temperature

2 eggs
1 cup buttermilk
2 cups cake flour
¼ teaspoon salt
¾ teaspoon baking soda

Preheat the oven to 350°F. Butter the cake pans.

Put the ginger into a food processor and process until it is in small bits, or chop fine by hand. Put the ginger and ¼ cup sugar in a small skillet or saucepan and cook over medium heat, stirring constantly until the sugar has melted and the mixture is warm (this takes only a minute or two). Set aside. Put the lemon pieces in the processor and process until finely chopped—or chop fine by hand. Add the lemon to the cooled ginger mixture.

Put the butter into a mixing bowl and beat a second or two; slowly add the remaining sugar and beat until smooth. Add the eggs and beat well. Stir in the buttermilk. Add the flour, salt, and baking soda and beat until smooth. Add the ginger-lemon mixture and mix well.

Spoon the batter into the buttered cake pans. Bake for 25 minutes. Remove from the oven and cool in the pans for 5 minutes, then turn out onto racks until completely cooled.

Soft Gingerbread

(one 8-inch square gingerbread)

This fine-crumbed and finely spiced gingerbread is exceptionally good.

1 cup sugar
1 cup dark molasses
1 cup vegetable oil
3 eggs
¾ teaspoon salt
1 teaspoon ground cloves

1 teaspoon ground ginger
1 teaspoon cinnamon
2 cups all-purpose flour
2 teaspoons baking soda
1 cup boiling water

Preheat the oven to 350°F. Grease and lightly flour the baking pan.

Put the sugar, molasses, oil, and eggs in a mixing bowl and beat until smooth. In another bowl, combine the salt, cloves, ginger, cinnamon, flour, and baking soda and stir with a fork until well mixed. Stir into the first mixture. Add the boiling water and beat briskly until smooth. This is a thin batter. Pour into the pan and bake 40 to 45 minutes. Serve warm.

Great Coffee Cake

(one 10-inch tube cake)

This makes a moist, rich cake adaptable to many changes. Some very good variations to this splendid basic cake follow the recipe.

½ pound (2 sticks) butter,
room temperature
1 cup sugar
3 eggs
2½ cups all-purpose flour

2 teaspoons baking powder
1 teaspoon baking soda
1 teaspoon salt
1 cup sour cream

Preheat the oven to 350°F. Grease and flour a 10-inch tube pan or Bundt pan.

Put the butter in a large mixing bowl and beat for several seconds. Add the sugar and beat until smooth. Add the eggs and beat for 2 minutes, or until light and creamy. Put the flour, baking powder, baking soda, and salt in a bowl and stir with a fork to blend well. Add the flour mixture to the butter mixture and beat until smooth. Add the sour cream and mix well.

Spoon the batter into the pan. Bake for about 50 minutes, or until a straw comes out clean when inserted into the center. Remove from the oven and let rest for 5 minutes in the pan. Invert onto a rack and cool a little bit before slicing. Serve warm.

Raisin and Spice Coffee Cake Add 1 teaspoon mace and 1 teaspoon nutmeg when combining the dry ingredients. Stir ¾ cup raisins and ½ cup currants into the batter after adding the sour cream, and proceed with the basic recipe.

Dried Fig and Almond Coffee Cake   You will need 1½ cups of Calimyrna figs; if the figs are very dry, put them in a bowl, pour boiling water over them, and let stand for 15 minutes; then drain. Cut the figs into quarters. After adding the sour cream, add these along with 1½ cups unblanched, coarsely chopped almonds. Stir well, and proceed with the basic recipe.

Apple and Walnut Coffee Cake   Add 1½ cups coarsely chopped apple (peeled or unpeeled) and 1½ cups coarsely chopped walnuts to the batter after adding the sour cream, and stir to distribute well. Proceed with the basic recipe.

Simple Vanilla Coffee Cake   Follow the basic recipe, but add 5 teaspoons vanilla extract when adding the sour cream.

Waverley found Miss Bradwardine presiding over the teas and coffee, the table loaded with warm bread, both of flour, oatmeal, and barley-meal, in the shape of loaves, cakes, biscuits, and other varieties, together with eggs, reindeer ham, mutton and beef ditto, smoked salmon, marmalade, and all other delicacies which induced even Johnson himself to extol the luxury of a Scotch breakfast above that of all other countries.

SIR WALTER SCOTT, *Waverley* (1841)

Fluffy Caramel Coffee Cake

(one 10-inch square cake)

The texture of this cake is indeed fluffy and light; and the topping is sticky, crisp caramel. The batter can be mixed and put in its baking dish in the refrigerator the night before you need it. When you get up in the morning, put the baking dish in the cold oven and turn on the heat. And serve with butter, of course.

1 package dry yeast
1/4 cup warm water
3/4 cup milk, approximately
2 tablespoons vegetable shortening
1/4 cup sugar
1/2 teaspoon salt
1 egg, beaten
2 cups all-purpose flour

Caramel topping
1 cup dark brown sugar
1/2 cup sour cream
1 teaspoon vanilla extract

Sprinkle the yeast over the warm water and allow to rest 5 minutes until it dissolves.

Put the milk and shortening in a small pan and heat, stirring together until the shortening melts. Transfer to a mixing bowl and stir in the sugar and salt until blended. Let the mixture cool, then add the dissolved yeast. Add the egg and mix well. Stir in the flour and mix until the dough is smooth. The dough should be slightly sticky; if it isn't, add 2 or 3 more tablespoons milk.

Grease the baking dish or pan. Spread the dough out in the pan by dipping your fingers in cold water (so the dough doesn't stick to your hands), then pat the dough evenly into the pan.

For the topping, stir together the brown sugar, sour cream, and vanilla in a small bowl until well blended. Cover the dough and let rise for about 1½ hours, or refrigerate overnight and bake in the morning.

Bake in a preheated 350°F oven for 15 minutes, then spread the topping over the cake. Bake an additional 20 minutes if the dough has risen at room temperature or bake an additional 30–35 minutes if the dough is chilled from resting overnight in the refrigerator.

Almond Coconut Coffee Cake

(three 8-inch twisted round cakes or three long twisted loaf cakes)

The lightly toasted almond and coconut in this rather flaky cake are very good. Long strips of unsweetened coconut, the best kind to use, can be found in natural food stores. The cake slices and toasts nicely and has a very fresh taste.

1 cup sliced or grated
   unsweetened coconut
1 cup sliced almonds
½ cup warm water
2 packages dry yeast
1 teaspoon plus ½ cup sugar
4 cups all-purpose flour
1 teaspoon salt
8 tablespoons (1 stick) butter,
   chilled
3 egg yolks
1 cup light cream

Topping
1½ cups confectioners' sugar
2 tablespoons water,
   approximately
½ cup coconut
½ cup sliced almonds

Spread 1½ cups coconut and 1½ cups almonds (for both the bread and the topping) on a baking sheet in a single layer. Put in the oven and turn the heat to 350°F. It will take about 10 minutes to toast the coconut and almonds to a light golden color, but check on the toasting process every couple of minutes so you don't burn them. Set aside.

Put the warm water in a large mixing bowl, sprinkle in the yeast and 1 teaspoon sugar, stir, and let dissolve for 5 minutes.

Put the flour, salt, and remaining ½ cup sugar in another bowl. Cut the cold butter into small pieces and add the flour mixture. Using your fingers or a pastry cutter, cut the butter into the flour mixture until it is in small bits.

Put the yolks and cream in a small bowl and beat until smooth and blended. Stir into the flour mixture. Add the yeast mixture and blend well. Add 1 cup each toasted coconut and almonds and mix to distribute.

Turn the dough onto a floured board (the dough will be slightly sticky), flour your hands, and divide the dough into 6 equal parts. Keeping your hands well floured, roll each piece into a rope 12 inches long. Twisting two ropes together at a time, make the coffee cakes either into long twisted loaves or into round twisted loaves. If you are making the round loaves, twist two ropes together, form a circle, pinch the ends together, and place the rounds on greased pie pans. Repeat with the remaining pieces of dough, to make three loaves altogether. If you are making long twisted loaves instead of rounds, bake them on greased baking sheets.

Let the cakes rise until double in bulk (this takes about 1½ hours). Bake in a preheated 350°F oven for about 35 minutes.

Stir together the confectioners' sugar and 2 tablespoons water to make the glaze. It should flow from the spoon; add a little more water if it doesn't. When you remove the cakes from the oven, spread the glaze over the cakes. Sprinkle the remaining ½ cup each toasted coconut and almonds over the frosting. Serve warm.

Apricot Prune Coffee Cake

(one 10-inch tube cake)

This is a large moist cake with brown sugar–walnut filling. It is always well liked and I've given away the recipe many times. Any dried fruit will do nicely in place of the apricots and prunes.

Brown Sugar Filling
1 cup brown sugar
1 teaspoon cinnamon
½ cup chopped walnuts

Cake Batter
1 cup finely chopped dried
   apricots
1 cup finely chopped pitted
   dried prunes
⅔ cup sugar
3 eggs
1 cup milk
½ cup (1 stick) butter, melted
2½ cups all-purpose flour
1 tablespoon baking powder
½ teaspoon salt

Preheat the oven to 350°F. Butter and flour a 10-inch tube pan or Bundt pan.

To make the filling, mix the brown sugar and cinnamon together in a small bowl, stirring with a fork until the cinnamon is well distributed. Stir in the walnuts and set aside.

Now make the cake batter. If the dried apricots and prunes are so dry that it is hard to chew them, put them in a bowl and pour boiling water over. Let stand for 10 minutes and drain, pressing out any excess water. Put the sugar, eggs, milk, and butter in a large mixing bowl and beat well. In another bowl, stir together the flour, baking powder, and salt to blend well. Stir the flour mixture into the sugar mixture, mixing until all ingredients are blended. Stir in the apricots and prunes.

Spread one third of the batter over the bottom of the prepared pan. Be sparing with the batter at this point. Spread half the brown sugar filling over the batter. Spread another third of the batter over the filling, then spread over the remaining brown sugar filling and top with the remaining batter.

Bake for 50 to 60 minutes, or until a straw comes out clean when inserted into the center. Remove from the oven and let cool for about 5 minutes in the pan. Carefully invert onto a rack to cool completely before slicing.

Condiments

Raw Fresh Fruit Jams
Peach Rose Jam
Rhubarb Ginger Jam
Strawberry Lump Preserves
Orange Marmalade
Orange Spread
Beet Marmalade
Lemon Jelly
   Orange Jelly
Lemonade Jelly with Orange Slices
Lemon Curd
Spicy Orange Slices
Lemon Pineapple Apple Relish
Date Raisin Condiment
Dried Apricot Orange Condiment
Papaya Pickle
Spice Walnuts
Caramel Oatmeal Topping
Maple Syrup Butter
Whipped Maple Syrup
Cinnamon Cream Syrup
English Custard
Salsa Verde
Homemade Yogurt
Breakfast Cheese

Here is a catch-all chapter for all the little side dishes that give an extra sprightliness to things we would otherwise eat plain. These small frills will give a little inspiration to a breakfast.

Some kind of fruit spread or jam always lends that extra dash to a piece of toast. Just as strawberry preserves seem to belong on white bread or biscuits, apple tastes wonderful on things like whole wheat and rye and pear jam belongs on things that are light and delicate. The idea of preserving fruit at home, however, has outlived its usefulness for most of us, partly because families are smaller and partly because so many things are available fresh. Moreover, people don't want to take the time for the all-day process of sterilizing jars, pressure cooking, and the rest. But you can easily have fresh jam by making it in small quantities — you'll need just a few pieces of fruit or a basket of berries.

I love the idea of raw fruit jams — there's nothing fresher and they are particularly appealing to those with a hectic routine. You can take something as small as one pear: peel it, add a little lemon juice and a little sugar, mash it in a bowl, and let it sit until the sugar dissolves. In just a little while, you will have made enough jam to tide you over a weekend of breakfasts.

Those of you who still take the time to make preserves the old-fashioned way will want to get a copy of *Fine Preserving*, by Catherine Plagemann, annotated by M. F. K. Fisher (Berkeley: Aris Books, 1986).

Raw Fresh Fruit Jams

(about two cups)

This is the very best, easiest, and most practical way to have splendid homemade jams on the table for each season. The fruit or berries must be properly ripe and mashable, and the texture of the jam should be coarse.

2 cups mashed fruit or berries
⅓ cup sugar (more or less,
    depending on sweetness
    desired)

Optional: lemon juice
    (if the fruit or berries are
    flat-tasting)

Put the fruit in a shallow dish, mash, and sprinkle the sugar and optional lemon juice over. Let the fruit sit until the sugar dissolves, about 30 minutes. Put in a pretty bowl and serve. Depending on the fruit used, the jam will keep anywhere from 3 days to 2 weeks, refrigerated.

Peach Rose Jam

(about two cups)

Rose water is available in pharmacies, labeled as Fluid Rose Soluble, at a reasonable price. Peach Rose Jam is heaven on wheat toast.

2 cups peeled, pitted, and coarsely
    mashed fresh peaches

Sugar to taste
3 or 4 drops rose water

Put the peaches and sugar in a skillet over low heat and stir the mixture for a minute, just long enough to melt and blend the fruit and sugar. Remove from the heat, cool, and carefully add the rose water to taste—the flavor should be a shy presence. The jam will keep about 3 days, refrigerated.

Rhubarb Ginger Jam

(four cups)

This jam has an arresting, different taste. It is splendid on rye or coarse wheat toast. The rhubarb flavor is not hindered by the piquant ginger.

About 2 pounds rhubarb, washed
  and cut into small pieces
  (to make 4 cups)
4 cups sugar (if tartness is desired,
  use only 3 cups)

¼ cup chopped unpeeled
  gingerroot

Put a layer of rhubarb in a shallow bowl, sprinkle with a layer of sugar, and continue layering until the last layer of rhubarb is covered with sugar. Cover the dish with plastic wrap and leave covered for 36 hours. Lots of juice will accumulate. Pour the juice into a saucepan. Tie the chopped ginger in a piece of muslin or cheesecloth. Put the ginger into the saucepan with the juice and boil for about 5 minutes. Add the rhubarb and simmer for about 15 minutes, or until the rhubarb begins to look translucent. Cool and transfer to sealed jars if storing for an indefinite time; or cover and refrigerate until needed. This will keep for a couple of weeks in the refrigerator, or a few months in the freezer.

Strawberry Lump Preserves

(1½ cups)

This method of making jam suits me just fine. You can add as much sugar as you wish and this recipe may be multiplied to any amount desired. It makes a bright red preserve and the full strawberry essence is captured in the lumps of strawberries. Strawberries are available for most of the summer, so I make the jam a little at a time.

About 4 cups (2 baskets) strawberries, washed, hulled, and sliced in half

½ cup sugar, approximately
½ cup fresh lemon juice

Choose a sunny, warm day to make this. Mash half the berries and put them in a sauté pan. Stir in the sugar and lemon juice and cook over medium-low heat for 1 or 2 minutes, stirring constantly. Add the rest of the halved strawberries. Turn the heat to medium and, still stirring constantly, bring the preserves to a boil. Spoon off the foam, let boil about 10 seconds more, and remove from the heat.

Pour the preserves into a large shallow dish so they are spread out in a thin layer. Cover the preserves with muslin or cheesecloth and put outdoors in the sunshine for at least 6 hours.

Spoon into jars and cover. Store in the refrigerator. If you want to keep these preserves longer than 10 days, put the jars in the freezer (remember to leave ½ inch of space in the jar).

Orange Marmalade

(three 8-ounce jars)

In some parts of England marmalade is called squish. Many commercial marmalades are so sweet that the orange flavor is lost, but you can make homemade marmalade to please yourself. The lemon in this recipe gives a nice tart edge to the marmalade.

3 large oranges	3 cups water
3 lemons	About 1½ cups sugar

Peel the oranges and two of the lemons, and cut the peel into very thin slices. Seed the oranges and cut up the pulp. Save the pulp of the two lemons for another use. Put the fruit and water in a pot. Bring to a boil and let simmer for 5 minutes. Remove from the heat and let stand overnight in a cool place.

Measure the fruit and liquid and, depending on your taste, add about ½ cup sugar for each cup fruit (you must add enough sugar to make the jam jell). Stir the sugar into the fruit and put the pot back on the stove over medium heat. Stirring often, let the jam cook about 30 minutes. Test for jell point by spooning a little jam onto a saucer and placing it in the refrigerator or freezer for a minute or two. If the jam jells it is ready to put into jars. I use the last lemon at this point. Peel the remaining lemon and slice the zest into very thin slices. Cut the pith away from the lemon and discard. Chop the lemon pulp into small pieces, remove any seeds, and add it and the zest to the jam.

Pour into three 8-ounce jars. If you seal the jars with paraffin, do so as follows. Leave ½ inch head space in the jar. Pour one thin layer of paraffin over the hot jam. Let this layer set until it is firm, and then pour on one more thin layer.

Orange Spread

(four servings)

A little stirring and cooking, and the result will be a warm, pleasing orange spread for your buttered toast.

¼ cup water	1 to 4 tablespoons sugar, to taste
1 tablespoon cornstarch	Pinch of salt
1 cup orange pulp and juice	

Dissolve the water and cornstarch together in a small saucepan, add the orange, and stir until blended. Cook over medium heat, stirring constantly, for 1 minute; then add the sugar and salt. Continue cooking and stirring until the mixture has thickened and become translucent. Remove from the heat and serve on buttered toast. This will keep for several days in the refrigerator. Just reheat when you are ready to use again.

Beet Marmalade

(three cups)

This will be the biggest surprise your taste buds have had in a long time — Beet Marmalade is absolutely delicious. Try spreading this marmalade on Crisp Whole Wheat Buns (see page 18) along with a layer of yogurt or sour cream.

4 medium-large beets, cooked and peeled	1 large lemon
1½ cups sugar	2 tablespoons chopped fresh ginger

Put the beets in a food processor and process until coarsely chopped; or mash the beets by hand. Transfer the beets to a heavy-bottomed saucepan and stir in the sugar.

Put the lemon and ginger into the food processor and process until finely chopped; or chop them by hand. Add the lemon and ginger to the beet mixture and stir to blend. Cook over medium-low heat, stirring often, until the marmalade has thickened a little. This takes about 20 minutes — remember that the marmalade will get thicker considerably as it cools.

Remove from the heat and put up in sterilized jars if you are not going to use the marmalade for a month or more; otherwise it will keep well in the refrigerator.

Lemon Jelly

(about one cup)

It's surprising that citrus jellies are not made more often. Fresh citrus fruits are available all year round, jellies are very easy to make, and they are delicious.

½ cup freshly squeezed
  lemon juice

1⅓ cups sugar
2 ounces pectin (1 box)

In a 3- or 4-quart saucepan, mix together the lemon juice, sugar, and pectin and bring to a boil, stirring at first to smooth and blend the ingredients. Allow to boil *exactly* 2 minutes and remove from the heat.

Wet a strong paper towel or a fine-textured dishcloth with cold water, wring out, and place the paper or cloth in a strainer over a Pyrex 2-cup measure. Let the jelly slowly drip through. Cool and seal, or cool and refrigerate.

Orange Jelly   Use ½ cup orange juice plus ¼ cup lemon juice and the grated zest of 1 orange (this is strained out after imparting its flavor).

Lemonade Jelly with Orange Slices

(about 2½ cups jelly)

Clean, sparkling lemonade jellied with fresh orange pieces: refreshing as snowflakes in July. Eat this with plain yogurt or buttered toast.

¼ cup cold water
1 tablespoon unflavored gelatin
1½ cups boiling water
¾ cup sugar, or to taste
Pinch of salt
6 tablespoons freshly squeezed
   lemon juice

Grated zest of 1 lemon
6 large oranges, peeled, sectioned,
   and membranes removed
Optional: a few sprigs of fresh
   mint

Put the cold water in a bowl and sprinkle the gelatin over; stir and let stand for 5 minutes until the gelatin has dissolved.

Pour the boiling water over the gelatin mixture, stir, and add the sugar, salt, lemon juice, and lemon zest. Stir until the sugar has dissolved and the lemonade is clear. Pour into individual molds or one large one. Cover, then refrigerate for about 4 to 6 hours.

Unmold and arrange with the orange sections and a leaf or two of fresh mint.

Lemon Curd

(two cups)

Slightly sweet and tartly lemon, this is a sunshine yellow preserve that spreads deliciously over toast or on a Whole Wheat Sponge Roll (see page 248). It will keep for a few weeks in the refrigerator or you can put it up in sterile jars to keep it longer.

Grated zest from 2 large lemons	8 tablespoons (1 stick) butter
6 tablespoons freshly squeezed	1 cup sugar
lemon juice	4 eggs

Put the zest, lemon juice, butter, and sugar in the top of a double boiler, or in a metal bowl, over simmering water (the water must not boil). Stir occasionally until the butter melts and the sugar dissolves. In a bowl, beat the eggs until thoroughly blended. Stirring constantly, spoon a little of the hot lemon mixture into the eggs. Pour the egg mixture into the bowl or pan, still stirring constantly, and continue to cook over the simmering water until the curd is thick. Remove from the heat and store in the refrigerator until needed.

Spicy Orange Slices

(about sixteen large orange slices)

Spicy Orange Slices are soaked in a very hot, rather thick, shiny glaze that is mildly spiced with cloves and cinnamon. Put a slice or two in a bowl and pile raspberries or strawberries on top; or cut up a slice and put the pieces on a hot buttered biscuit or scone. These are very good with Pork Tenderloin with Biscuits and Gravy (see page 196).

3 oranges	¼ cup water
2 cups sugar	10 whole cloves
½ cup vinegar	1 stick cinnamon

Cut each orange into 5 or 6 slices and discard the end pieces. Set aside.

Put the sugar, vinegar, water, cloves, and cinnamon in a sauté pan. Bring to a boil and boil about 3 minutes, or until the syrup thickens slightly.

Remove the pan from the heat. Put as many orange slices as the pan will hold in a single layer. Turn them over so each gets a thorough coating of glaze. Place the glazed slices in a bowl and continue to soak and coat all the remaining slices. Pour the remaining syrup over them. Cover and refrigerate, and use as needed. They will keep for 2 weeks in the refrigerator.

Lemon Pineapple Apple Relish

(five cups)

This relish is a pleasing merger of tastes. Serve it with ham, or spread it over toast and serve with a bowl of oatmeal.

2 cups coarsely chopped fresh
   pineapple
2 cups peeled, coarsely chopped
   apple
1/3 cup seeded and ground
   lemon pulp

3/4 cup sugar (depending on
   how sweet the pineapple and
   apples are)

Put the pineapple, apple, lemon, and sugar in a heavy-bottomed sauté pan. Turn the heat to medium-low and stir until the sugar dissolves and the juices run a little. Turn the heat to low and cook for about 30 minutes, stirring every now and then. Let the relish cool in the pan. Put in jars and seal if you are keeping it indefinitely, or put in covered containers and refrigerate until needed. This relish will keep for 10 days in the refrigerator.

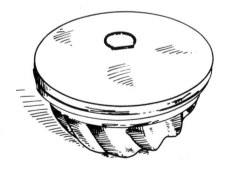

Date Raisin Condiment

(2½ cups)

This Date Raisin Condiment makes a fine spread on toast or on a breakfast sandwich made with a rather tart cheese. It is also a good filling for stuffed dates for a breakfast fruit plate.

1 cup pitted and coarsely ground dates	1 cup coarsely chopped walnuts
½ cup ground raisins	1 tablespoon lemon juice
½ cup ground currants	3 tablespoons water
	2 tablespoons honey

Put the ingredients in a bowl and mix thoroughly. Keep in the refrigerator until needed; this will keep for several weeks.

Dried Apricot Orange Condiment

(1¼ cups)

This is to be eaten with gusto—on toast, stirred into a hot cereal, or over oatmeal pancakes. Measure the ingredients carefully, and taste critically to be sure the balance is just right.

½ cup orange juice	1 cup coarsely ground dried apricots
1 tablespoon lemon juice	⅓ cup ground orange rind
6 tablespoons sugar	

Put the orange juice, lemon juice, and sugar in a small, heavy-bottomed pan. Cook over medium heat until the sugar is dissolved. Stir in the apricots and orange rind and cook, continuing to stir, for several minutes, or until the mass gets thick. Let cool and store in a jar in the refrigerator. Seal if you are preserving for more than 10 days.

Papaya Pickle

(two cups)

This breakfast pickle can spruce up a plate of ham or hash. The papaya seeds give a peppery taste and a nice snap to the pickle.

1 cup water
1 cup sugar
1/2 cup cider vinegar
1/4 teaspoon freshly ground
   pepper
3 whole cloves

2-inch stick cinnamon
2 bay leaves
1 firm, ripe papaya, peeled,
   seeded (reserve 2 tablespoons
   seeds), and cut into bite-size
   cubes

Put the water, sugar, vinegar, pepper, cloves, cinnamon stick, bay leaves, and papaya seeds in a saucepan and bring to a boil. Reduce the heat and simmer for 10 minutes. Add the papaya cubes and simmer for 30 minutes more.

Remove from the heat and let cool in the pan. Put into jars with lids and refrigerate or, if serving the same day, place in a bowl and serve at room temperature. Papaya Pickle will keep for 2 weeks in the refrigerator.

Spice Walnuts

(2½ cups)

A small mound of Spice Walnuts, Breakfast Cheese (see page 286), figs, toast, and tea make a choice breakfast in bed. These crisp, sweet walnuts go well with many breakfast custards, or with ham and fruit.

2½ cups walnut halves (or large pieces)	1 teaspoon cinnamon
1 cup sugar	1 teaspoon salt
½ cup water	Optional: 1 tablespoon vanilla extract

Preheat the oven to 350°F.

Spread the walnuts in one layer on a baking sheet. Roast in the oven for 10 to 15 minutes (watch carefully—nuts scorch easily), until the nuts become a little toasted, or lightly browned.

Put the sugar, water, cinnamon, and salt in a heavy-bottomed saucepan. You will be cooking until the soft-ball (or spin-a-thread) stage (236°F). Let the syrup cook without stirring about 10 minutes. You will notice that the bubbles will become smaller and more compact as the syrup nears the soft-ball stage. Remove from the heat, stir in the vanilla, if using, and add the walnuts. Stir the mixture slowly and gently until it is creamy. Turn onto a buttered platter and separate the walnuts. Allow to cool and serve, or store in an airtight container.

Caramel Oatmeal Topping

(about three cups)

Sprinkle Caramel Oatmeal Topping over applesauce, cooked cereal, or baked bananas.

8 tablespoons (1 stick) butter
1 cup dark brown sugar
1 teaspoon vanilla extract

¼ teaspoon salt
2 cups uncooked oatmeal

Preheat the oven to 325°F. Mix the butter, brown sugar, vanilla, and salt in a small saucepan over low heat, stirring constantly until the sugar has dissolved.

Put the oatmeal in a bowl, pour the melted caramel sauce over, and toss the mixture until the oatmeal is coated with sauce. Spread the oatmeal in a thin layer on a baking sheet. Bake for 20 minutes, stirring the oatmeal once or twice. Remove from the oven and cool. Store in an airtight container.

MAPLE SYRUP

Real maple syrup is so much better than the maple-flavored pancake syrups that I strongly recommend you give it a try. It is graded according to color and strength: Grade A is divided into Light Amber, Medium Amber, and Dark Amber; and Grade B is the darkest. The lighter the syrup the more delicate and subtle the maple flavor. For some breakfast dishes, you may prefer the rich robust taste of Grade B. Real maple syrup is expensive, so here are two recipes to help get the most out of its incomparable flavor.

Maple Syrup Butter

(one cup)

You might not think that you could extend your maple syrup without diluting its flavor, but this recipe is not just economical, it actually enriches and rounds out the pure maple taste.

½ cup maple syrup
½ cup water

4 tablespoons (½ stick) unsalted butter

Put the syrup, water, and butter in a small saucepan and heat until the butter has melted. Stir to blend, and serve. Refrigerate any that is left over.

Whipped Maple Syrup

(about three cups)

This is a delectable topping for waffles, pancakes, muffins, fruits, or any dish that needs a pretty finish.

½ cup maple syrup
¼ cup water
2 egg whites

1 teaspoon lemon juice
½ cup heavy cream, whipped

Mix together the maple syrup and water in a small, heavy-bottomed saucepan. Bring to a boil, turn the heat to medium, and let the syrup boil for about 5 minutes, or until it forms the soft-ball (or spin-a-thread) stage (236°F on a candy thermometer). While the syrup is boiling, beat the egg whites with the lemon juice until the whites are stiff but still moist. When the syrup has reached the proper point, slowly beat the syrup into the egg whites. When the syrup is thoroughly mixed with the whites, fold in the whipped cream.

This mixture keeps well (although it does lose some of its air) for a few days. Stir it well before you use it to combine the liquid on the bottom with the lighter mixture on top.

Cinnamon Cream Syrup

(1⅓ *cups*)

Cinnamon Cream Syrup is a smooth and creamy topping with a mild cinnamon taste that goes well with Brown Rice Pancakes (see page 124) or Buckwheat Pancakes (see page 123). It is very rich, so a little bit goes a long way. Keep it in the refrigerator, and reheat as needed.

5 tablespoons butter	3 tablespoons sugar
1 cup heavy cream	1 teaspoon cinnamon

Melt the butter in a small saucepan and stir in the cream, sugar, and cinnamon. Whisking constantly, cook until the sugar has melted and the syrup is hot, about 1½ minutes.

English Custard

(two cups)

Don't be fooled by the word custard. English Custard is really a smooth sauce with the consistency of heavy cream—a pouring custard. This will give just the right finish to the stewed rhubarb on page 174, or any stewed fruit, and it is delicious with Lemon Pound Cake (see page 249) or Indian Loaf Cake (see page 252). Practice making this a few times and it will be in your permanent repertoire.

2 cups milk
½ cup sugar
4 egg yolks, lightly beaten
    with a fork

⅛ teaspoon salt
2 teaspoons vanilla extract

Heat the milk in a heavy-bottomed saucepan to the simmer point (a film begins to form on top of the milk, bubbles appear around the edges of the pan, and steam starts to rise from the milk). Remove from the heat, add the sugar, and stir a few minutes to dissolve. Pour a little of the hot milk over the yolks, stirring briskly. Add the yolk mixture to the milk, return to the heat, add the salt, and cook over low heat, stirring constantly. After a few minutes pay close attention and keep stirring; when you feel a slight thickening of the custard, remove from the heat (it will be a thin sauce). Pour into a bowl through a sieve or strainer, add the vanilla, and stir a few seconds until the custard is cool. It will thicken somewhat as it cools. Serve either warm or chilled.

Salsa Verde

(about one cup)

Salsa Verde is as zingy and peppy as a mariachi band. This is the only recipe in this book that contains garlic and onions, which are not my idea of breakfast ingredients, but it is so particularly good with thin cornmeal pancakes and delicious spooned over scrambled eggs or an omelet that I couldn't leave it out.

3 large cloves garlic
2 tablespoons cilantro, approximately
1 small jalapeño pepper, seeded

½ medium onion
6 tomatillos
½ teaspoon salt

Finely chop by hand the garlic, cilantro, jalapeño pepper, onion, and tomatillos. Mix them together in a bowl with the salt. Or put all of the ingredients in a food processor and process until coarsely chopped. This sauce will keep in the refrigerator for 3 or 4 days.

Homemade Yogurt

(one quart)

This is Judith Jones's recipe for making yogurt. Homemade yogurt is easy to make and less expensive than store-bought. Yogurt all by itself is a quick and nourishing breakfast.

You can make flavored yogurt yourself that will taste better than the flavored yogurts you can buy in the market by adding fresh fruits and berries, or preserves, or grated lemon zest (for lemon yogurt).

1 quart milk
2 tablespoons fresh plain yogurt

Heat 1 quart milk to the boiling point for just 1 minute. Cool to 115°F. Gently stir in 2 tablespoons fresh plain yogurt (the starter) and pour into a crockery or glass bowl. Cover snugly with plastic wrap and set in a warm spot. An oven with just its pilot light on or its electric light burning is ideal. Or put it in a warm corner of the kitchen with a blanket draped over to protect it from drafts. The yogurt should be ready in about 5 to 8 hours—tilt the bowl to see if it holds together. It should then be chilled 3 hours to firm up even more. If the yogurt sets for too long a time or if you use too much starter, it will be watery. It will keep refrigerated for about a week.

Breakfast Cheese

(1½ *cups*)

This is exactly the cheese I've always wanted to make at home—firm enough to be spreadable and with a good, clean, wholesome taste. It is slightly sour and whips into a very smooth creaminess. You may double or triple this recipe with good results. Carlie Stillman shared this with me and she said it came from Jack Lirio—thank you both a lot.

1 quart milk
½ cup cultured buttermilk

Mix the milk and buttermilk together in a stainless-steel or glass bowl and choose a larger pot that will contain it. Cover the bowl with plastic wrap and let stand at room temperature at least one full day.

Fill the large pot with very hot tap water and place the bowl with the milk mixture inside. After 2 to 3 minutes, water will begin to appear around the edges of the mixture. Turn the heat on, start timing, and heat for 5 minutes, keeping the water just below a boil. A white, curdy mass will form. Remove the pot from the water bath, put it on a rack, and cool for 1 to 2 hours.

Ladle the contents of the pot into cheesecloth or a fine strainer set over a bowl. Drain for at least 2 hours. Put the cheese in a jar and refrigerate. It will keep for about 2 weeks refrigerated.

Breakfast Beverages

Tea

Tea is a splendid breakfast beverage, and a little tea knowledge can give you a great cup of tea. Many people believe that tea goes better than coffee with most breakfast dishes. For breakfast, most tea drinkers prefer strong, hearty black teas that mix well with milk. There are English Breakfast and Irish Breakfast blends, and one called simply Breakfast Tea that is blended in Scotland. The classic breakfast tea is considered by many to be Keemun, a Chinese black tea that has a bouquet that reminds them of hot fresh toast. Green teas are good with rice porridge or with a bowl of farina and a coddled egg, but should not be drunk with milk. Lapsang Souchong, a black China tea with a strong smoky flavor, goes well with very savory breakfast foods, especially smoked meat and fish. The scented teas like Earl Grey (flavored with bergamot, giving it a citrus taste), jasmine tea, or Constant Comment (*strongly* flavored with spices and orange peel) can clash with anything other than the plainest breakfast foods.

When buying tea, try to get loose leaves, not tea bags: the tea will probably taste better. Store tea in a tea caddy or other airtight container, and keep it in a dark and dry place; tea shouldn't be kept in the refrigerator.

It is easy to make a good cup of tea. Use fresh, cold water, and bring it to a rolling boil. Have on hand a clean, warm teapot—earthenware, not metal—heated with hot tap water or just kept in a warm place. Add ½ to 1 teaspoon tea leaves to the pot for every 6-ounce cup. The keenest flavor is extracted when the water is at a full rolling boil, so the old rule "bring the pot to the kettle, not the kettle to the pot" makes sense. Pour the boiling water over the tea, stir once, cover, and steep for 3 to 5 minutes. Then pour out the tea into your teacups through a tea strainer, unless you don't mind a few tea leaves in the bottom of your cup. A tea ball can be a great convenience. The big, stainless-steel mesh kind is best (only half fill the tea ball): more water circulates through them and they don't lend any metallic taste to the tea.

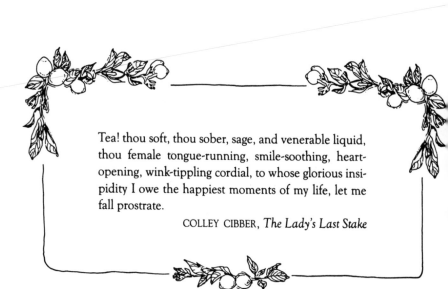

Tea! thou soft, thou sober, sage, and venerable liquid, thou female tongue-running, smile-soothing, heart-opening, wink-tippling cordial, to whose glorious insipidity I owe the happiest moments of my life, let me fall prostrate.

COLLEY CIBBER, *The Lady's Last Stake*

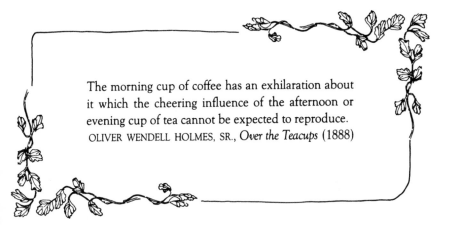

The morning cup of coffee has an exhilaration about it which the cheering influence of the afternoon or evening cup of tea cannot be expected to reproduce.
OLIVER WENDELL HOLMES, SR., *Over the Teacups* (1888)

Coffee

If you can afford the time, you can become a real coffee connoisseur, choosing your own beans and grinding, even roasting, them yourself. If you do, you will make a terrific cup of coffee. But you can also have a first-rate cup made from vacuum-packed canned coffee. For my electric drip machine, I usually use a blend of two brand-name coffees: a normal supermarket drip grind and an espresso-type dark roast. Coffee should be stored airtight in the refrigerator or freezer; you don't have to let it thaw out to use it.

There are a few things you should know to make a good cup of coffee. Don't let the coffee boil while it is being made, and don't let the coffee stay too long at a high temperature or try to reheat it: the coffee will taste harsh and bitter. I always pour my coffee as soon as it is made from the drip machine pot into a thermos jug: in it the coffee stays hot and fresh-tasting for hours. The general rule for regular strength coffee is to use 2 tablespoons coffee for each 8-ounce cup water. The cup markings on the side of your coffee maker will probably be for 6-ounce cups, or smaller, so adjust accordingly. To make very strong coffee, use more; brewing it longer will make it stronger but not better. To make it weaker, it is better to dilute it with hot water rather than using less coffee.

Hot Chocolate

(one cup)

This is the only method I have ever used to make hot chocolate. It is quite delicious and well balanced, so I've looked no further.

¼ cup water
1½ tablespoons cocoa

2 teaspoons sugar, or to taste
¾ cup milk

Put the water, cocoa, and sugar in a small saucepan over medium heat, and stir constantly until the mixture is smooth. Let it boil for a few seconds and slowly add the milk, stirring constantly. When the cocoa gets very hot, serve.

Mexican Chocolate   Add ⅛ teaspoon cinnamon to each cup, or put a 2-inch cinnamon stick in the saucepan when you are adding the milk.

ORANGE JUICE

A pitcher or a glass of fresh juice on the table is as nice as sunshine coming through the window. There is something very cheering about a glass of bright orange juice that has a sparkle to it—it just looks nice. Even if I don't drink it, I like to see orange juice on the breakfast table.

Cuban Orange Juice

(one glass)

One nice thing about this simple orange juice and milk drink is that if you add the optional egg, you won't detect any unpleasant raw eggy taste.

½ cup orange juice
½ cup milk
Optional: 1 egg

Put the orange juice, milk, and egg, if desired, in a blender. Blend until smooth and frothy, and serve cold.

Cold or Hot Lemonade

(one ten-ounce glass)

You might not think to have lemonade at your breakfast table; however, it is not only refreshing but a good way to get your vitamin C. Hot lemonade has always been considered a curative, and cold lemonade is just right for those hot summer mornings when your brow is dripping.

2 tablespoons freshly squeezed
   lemon juice
1½ to 2 tablespoons sugar syrup*

8 ounces water (soda water is
   sometimes refreshing)

*NOTE: To make sugar syrup, bring equal amounts sugar and water to a boil, stir, and remove from the heat. Cool before using.

For cold lemonade, put the lemon juice, sugar syrup, and water in a glass and stir. Add ice for the chill. For hot lemonade, add boiling water to the lemon juice and sugar syrup, stir, and serve.

Banana Milk

(one glass)

I drank Banana Milk all one spring when I had to hurry to class and didn't have time to linger in the kitchen. It is thick, fresh, and filling.

1 ripe banana, peeled
Pinch of nutmeg
¾ cup milk

Put the banana, nutmeg, and milk in a blender and whip until the mixture is smooth and light.

Garden Tomato Juice

(one twelve-ounce glass)

You will need a blender to make this, but you don't have to fuss with the tomatoes and peel and seed them. Bottled or canned tomato juice is as different from fresh tomato juice as Spam from ham. This is a frothy glass of garden tomato.

2 medium tomatoes
⅓ cup water
Salt and pepper to taste

Trim the stem away from the tomatoes and put them into a blender with the water. Blend for a minute, add salt and pepper to taste, and blend again until well mixed.

Airy Eggnog

(one eight-ounce cup)

This is a billow of air, an innocent eggnog without a drop of liquor.

1 egg, separated
About ⅛ teaspoon ground or
   freshly grated nutmeg

½ cup milk
About 1 tablespoon sugar syrup*

*NOTE: To make sugar syrup, bring equal amounts sugar and water to a boil, stir, and remove from the heat. Cool before using.

Put the egg yolk, nutmeg, and milk in a small bowl and beat until the mixture is pale and a little foamy (I use a hand-rotary beater). Add the sugar syrup and beat until blended.

Beat the egg white until stiff but moist: the peaks should be just holding upright. With a spoon, gently stir the beaten egg white into the yolk mixture until mixed. Taste and add a bit more nutmeg or sugar syrup if desired.

Malted Milk

(one eight-ounce glass)

Where has malt gone? I remember rich, thick chocolate malts that completely fulfilled any hungry cravings. I felt like purring after downing one of these cold, fluffy concoctions. These days when you order a malt, you get a mix of vanilla ice cream, chocolate syrup, and thin milk—so skimpy, and devoid of malt flavor. You can buy malt in the supermarket and make one perfect drink in the old style. One of these will probably tide you over until dinner, and the addition of ice cream makes it ideal.

Any of the following additions to your malt would be delicious: a scoop of vanilla or chocolate ice cream; a peeled, ripe banana; or a cup of washed, trimmed berries or peeled, pitted fruit.

2½ tablespoons malt
⅔ cup milk

Put the malt and the milk in a blender and whip until smooth and frothy.

Fruit Juice Food

(one eight-ounce glass)

Foods that are good for you often don't taste good, but I think you will find this to be quite refreshing and pleasing.

⅓ cup apple juice
⅓ cup skim (or whole) milk
2 teaspoons maple syrup
1 tablespoon wheat germ

3 tablespoons nonfat dry milk
2 tablespoons bran
2 ice cubes

Put all of the ingredients in a blender and blend until frothy. Drink cold.

Breakfast Menus

A SPECIAL BIRTHDAY

Grapefruit Juice
Cream Biscuits
Breakfast Steak
Rough and Ready Potatoes
The Coach House Bread and Butter Pudding

×

Baked Pineapple
Pork Tenderloin with Biscuits and Gravy
Madeira Poppy Seed Cake

EASTER BREAKFAST

Fresh Berries
Lemon Zephyrs
Fresh Ginger Cake

THANKSGIVING BREAKFAST

Ham
Pumpkin Mush
Ballymaloe Baked Breakfast Fruit

CHRISTMAS BREAKFAST

Fresh Fruit and Melon
Pulled Bread
Buttermilk Barley Biscuits
Kedgeree
Cranberry Raisin Pie

NEW YEAR'S

Brown Scones
Ham
Buttermilk Baked Eggs
Baked Stuffed Pears
Whole Wheat Sponge Roll

WINTER

Cranberry Poached Apples
Eggs Beatrice
Steamed Persimmon Pudding

×

Creamed Chipped Beef with Mushrooms
Boston Brown Bread Muffins
Baked Pineapple

×

Bannocks
Beet Marmalade
Scrambled Eggs with Ham

Applesauce
Soft Gingerbread
Tea

×

Orange Juice
Spice Walnuts
Breakfast Cheese
Dates and Figs
Toasted Raisin Cinnamon Wheat Bread

SPRING

Fresh Peaches and Berries
Custard-Filled Cornbread
Breakfast Sausage

×

Fresh Grapefruit
Trout Fried with Oatmeal
Hash Browns

×

Fresh Grapefruit Juice Ice
Sharlotka

×

Fresh Orange with Marmalade
Cheese Bannocks

×

Featherbed Eggs with Fresh Fruit and Cream Cheese
Raw Apple Muffins

×

Melon
Calas
Hot Chocolate

SUMMER

Fresh Ripe Mango
Bridge Creek Fresh Ginger Muffins
Oatmeal Soufflé

×

Tea
Rhubarb with English Custard
Ginger Shortbread

×

Sliced Plums with Yogurt
Knothole Eggs
Bacon

×

Fresh Berries
Bridge Creek Heavenly Hots
Bacon

Inside-out Mango
Ginger Pancakes
Green Mango Fool

×

Melon
Crisp Whole Wheat Buns
Buttermilk Baked Eggs

×

Garden Tomato Juice
Creamed Mushroom Toast

×

Fresh Peaches
Brown Barley
Lemon Yogurt Muffins

FALL

Fresh Papaya with Seeds and Lime
Good Grits
Fried Eggs Sunny-Side-Up
Bacon
White Toast

×

Chinese Tea Eggs
Rice Cereal
Persimmons

Salt Cod Cakes
Shirred Lemon Eggs
Melba Toast

×

White Cornbread with Sage
Ham Loaf
Fried Apple Rings

×

Pink Grapefruit Apple Dish
Homemade Yogurt
Boston Brown Bread Muffins

×

Scotch Eggs
Melba Toast
Ballymaloe Baked Breakfast Fruit

×

Orange Juice
Goldenrod Eggs
Ruffled Ham

A SPECIAL DAY

Fresh Pineapple
Thin Yellow Cornmeal Pancakes
Salsa Verde
Mexican Chocolate

A DAY IN BED

Baked Banana
Milk Toast (Oven)

BREAKFAST IN BED

Ham and Farm Cheese Butter-Fried Sandwich
Baked Apple

×

Cuban Orange Juice
Pulled Bread
Figs with Breakfast Cheese

ANYTIME BREAKFAST

Pink Grapefruit Apple Dish
Butter-Basted Eggs
Oatmeal Biscuits

×

Fresh Grapefruit
Peerless Cornbread Muffins
Shirred Eggs with Bacon

A SPECIAL BREAKFAST

Fresh Lemon Juice Ice
Hard-Boiled Eggs
Smoked Salmon Toast

✕

Baked Stuffed Pears
Sherry and Ginger Steamed Pudding

✕

Fresh Orange and Cranberry Compote
Toasted Buttered Slices of Pound Cake

✕

Malted Milk
Crumpets with Peach Rose Jam

A VERY, VERY SPECIAL BREAKFAST

Fresh Orange Juice Ice
Chocolate Walnut Butter Bread French Toast

Index

A NOTE ABOUT THE AUTHOR

Marion Cunningham was born in Southern California and now lives in Walnut Creek. She was responsible for the complete revision of *The Fannie Farmer Cookbook* and is the author of the Wings Great Cookbooks, *The Fannie Farmer Baking Book* and *The Supper Book*. She travels frequently throughout the country giving cooking demonstrations, has contributed articles to *Bon Appétit, Food & Wine,* and *Gourmet* magazines, and writes a column for the San Francisco *Chronicle* and the Los Angeles *Times*. She also has been a consultant to a number of well-known West Coast restaurants.

A NOTE ON THE TYPE

The text of this book has been set in Goudy Old Style, one of the more than a hundred typefaces designed by Frederic William Goudy (1865–1947). Although Goudy began his career as a bookkeeper, he was so inspired by the appearance of several newly published books from the Kelmscott Press that he devoted the remainder of his life to typography in an attempt to bring a better understanding of the movement led by William Morris to the printers of the United States.

Produced in 1914, Goudy Old Style reflects the absorption of a generation of designers with things "ancient." Its smooth, even color, combined with its generous curves and ample cut, marks it as one of Goudy's finest achievements.

Designed by Dorothy Schmiderer
and Claire M. Naylon